# Nellie

## A Darlaston Wench

*This book is dedicated to my parents, my late husband Derek and our three girls, Margaret, Katherine and Jennifer*

———◆•◆◆•◆———

*With special thanks to Carl and Jean for their help and encouragement*

# Nellie

## A DARLASTON WENCH

Marion Rowley

THE HISTORY PRESS

First published in the United Kingdom in 2009 by
The History Press
The Mill · Brimscombe Port · Stroud · Gloucestershire · GL5 2QG

British Library Cataloguing in Publication Data
A catalogue record for this book is available from the British Library.

ISBN 978-0-7509-5116-6

Typeset in 11/13pt Sabon
Typesetting and origination by
The History Press.
Printed and bound in England.

# Contents

*Nellie, Annie, Martha and Joe at the seaside, c. 1933.*

# Foreword

## *by Professor Carl Chinn MBE*

Born on Sunday 8 July 1906, Ellen Leah White, née Askey and better known as Nellie, was proud of coming from and belonging to a working-class Darlaston family. Her daughter, Marion Rowley of Sedgley, thoughtfully sent me her mother's account of the lives of the people of her town from 1906 until the 1930s. She told me 'my late mother had total recall of those years and I made several tapes, one of which the Black Country Society was happy to add to their archives. It is very important to me that her accounts of those times are not lost to a new generation.' I agree with Marion's sentiments and I am honoured that she has shared with me her Mum's words; for this memoir is unlike most life stories that are written in literary language and can sometimes be stilted and distant from their subjects. By contrast it sets down the speech of Nellie and the people to whom she belonged in a simple, vital and compelling way.

As such it has a power to engage us with the everyday life of one family, but through whose actions, thoughts and expressions we catch hold of shared values, shared identities, and shared experiences. Herein lies the vigour of Nellie's story: for all that it is hers it is our too. In harking at her words we hear once again our grans and grandads, our moms and dads, our uncles and aunts, their neighbours, and all those who toiled and moiled through the tough times of the inter-war years, hoping, one day that their children or their children's children would have a better life. Through Nellie's eyes we see the streets not only of industrial Darlaston but also of the industrial West Midlands, and through her soul we feel the stirring of all those who suffered want and adversity in a wealthy land and still strove to stay proud, clean and respectable.

Nellie pulls us into a tough working-class life in which you had to lie on your bed and make it as best as you could; and yet for all that poverty was a fact of life. Nellie and her people did not live in isolation seeking only to look after themselves. Selfishness was a sin they knew not. In spite of privation and family fallouts they clung to kin and neighbours and forged strong ties to one another. They had to, for there was precious little help from the rich or the state. Working people had to make do and mend. And make do and mend they did through reaching out to each other and adopting as many coping strategies as they could in the face of that hard enemy called poverty. Crucially their world was not one of me and mine, it was a world of us and ours. This then is the story of the earliest memories of Nellie: A Darlaston Wench, the daughter of Annie and Jim Askey who always held fast to the principles instilled into her by her people and whose words now keep her people alive though they be long gone.

# 1

# 'A Bonny Little Gel'

The old midwife held up the newly born infant by the ankles, giving it a smart tap on its bottom. At first it remained inert, as if reluctant to fill its lungs with the air of the world it had just entered. Another slap administered by Nurse Shaw persuaded it to open its mouth and bawl lustily in protest.

'There you are Annie, her's right as nine pence and by God her's a big 'un.' Nurse turned to smile reassuringly at the strained face of the anxious mother before carefully weighing the baby.

'What did I tell you, 12lb 10oz, not as heavy as George – he was 14lb if I remember right – but this one's a bonny little gel.'

After washing the baby and wrapping her tightly in a shawl, Nurse Shaw placed the snuffling infant into its mother's arms.

'Now I'll just tidy round a bit', she said, 'and Jim can pop up and see you, then I must see about getting home.'

Nurse Shaw glanced at her watch, noted that the time was 12.15 and hoped that her Sunday roast was being attended to.

'Would you open the window, please,' asked Annie faintly, pushing back dark strands of hair from her hot forehead. Nurse moved obligingly to the window, pushing it up with difficulty. The fresh summer breeze entered the stuffy, sickly-smelling room behind her as she leaned out for a moment, looking up and down Station Street, noticing a handful of ragged urchins squatting on the hot, dusty blue bricks. Footsteps passed directly underneath the window, and leaning further out, Nurse Shaw saw that it was Jim Askey, who had slipped out for a much needed pint.

'There's Jim, Annie, I'll just give him a shout!'

She bustled to the door and in response to her call there was a heavy tread upon the uncarpeted stairs and a moment later Jim poked his head a little nervously round the door.

'It is all over then?' he asked.

'It is, Jim', beamed Nurse, 'and you've got a lovely little girl, her's a whopper, 12lb 10oz.'

Jim's eyes met his wife's questioningly as he moved over to the bed. 'You all right, Annie?'

'Course I am', she replied, adjusting the shawl so that he could get a good look at his new daughter.

'It weren't half as bad as when our George was born', she continued, 'd'yer remember what it was like when we had him?'

Did he indeed, Jim was never likely to forget. He was a bricklayer and had been out of work for sixteen weeks because of heavy frost and then he'd been kicked by Charlie Simmonds' horse, breaking a leg. There was no unemployment money then and they had survived on a diet of swedes and dripping supplied by an old aunt of Jim's. When George was born Annie had been attended by Nurse Shaw and she would always be grateful to that kind old lady who had brought her a basin of gruel and refused the 2s 6d Annie had saved to pay for her confinement.

Times were a little easier now, eighteen months later. Jim had regular employment and could afford to feed his small family adequately. He turned to the nurse who, having finished her ministrations, was making ready to leave.

*The Vine.*

'How heavy did'st say her was?'

'12lb 10oz,' she replied somewhat surprised by the sudden interest in his daughter's weight.

'Well you see, I've just heard 'Lijah Brown down at the Vine braggin' about the baby his missus has just 'ad and it was only 5 lb!'

''Ere then,' Nurse Shaw reached over and took the baby from its mother's arms, handing it to Jim.

'You tek her down and let 'em have a look at this one. I reckon you'm got sommat to brag about!'

And so it was that on Sunday 8 July 1906, when Ellen Leah, later to be known as Nellie, was less than two hours old, she was placed on the counter of the Vine and toasted by Jim and his pals and a slightly subdued Mr Brown.

# 2

# Coronation Day

Nellie sat on the Mission wall in a state of confusion and excitement. She was now nearly five years old and barely able to comprehend what all the noise and cheering was about. That morning her mother had combed her hair and, dividing it into two bunches, had tied them tightly with red, white and blue ribbons. Her face had been subjected to a vigorous scrubbing until it shone like a shiny little apple. She wore her best red plaid dress with the sailor collar, covered by a crisply starched, white pinafore. Seven-year-old George had also received his mother's special attention, protesting loudly at the scrubbing and the tight uncomfortable celluloid collar, which bit into his neck.

'Do I 'ave to wear this, mother?' he pleaded, rubbing a finger inside the collar.

'Yes, yer do,' insisted Annie, 'an' it's no good goin' on neither. I reckon as all the rest o' the kids'll be dressed up today, so shut up moanin'.'

Once the children were attired to her satisfaction, Annie set Nellie on the kitchen table in order to fasten the tiny buttons on her boots, then lifting her down, she turned to George.

'Tek Nellie down to the school as quick as you can, they'm givin' all the children a present or somethin' today so mek haste or there'll be nothin' left.'

George had needed no second bidding. Holding his little sister's hand tightly, he pulled her out of the dark kitchen into the brilliant sunshine outside.

There had been an unusual number of folks about that morning. Women stood on their freshly ochred doorsteps to gossip. The houses were gay with bunting and there was a general atmosphere of excitement.

When Nellie and George arrived at the steps of the little Mission School, which Nellie had begun to attend when she was just three-and-a-half years old, numbers of their schoolmates, all presenting an

*The Askey children.*

*Annie with Nellie, Tom, George and Evelyn.*

unfamiliar clean and tidy appearance, jostled with each other when requested by the teacher to form an orderly queue. Along with the others, Nellie received a celebration mug, a medal and an orange. Carrying these carefully she had followed George home and as they turned the corner into Heath Road, her mother had been waiting anxiously, in case the children should spoil their best clothes.

Jim arrived home early from work that day along with some of his mates and he now stood behind Nellie, his hands encircling her plump waist, in case she should slip from the wall. She wouldn't realise until she was older that all the excitement, cheering and the procession she was about to witness on that June day in 1911, were in celebration of the Coronation of King George V. Annie, Jim and Grandad Tom remained seated on the wall with the children, chatting to a few neighbours, long after the general crowd had dispersed. Nellie climbed onto her grandad's lap and laid her head against his waistcoat. She could hear the faint tick, tick of his pocket watch and as his arms moved to settle her more comfortably, the heat of the afternoon sun on her uncovered head and the steady ticking of the watch combined to make her feel drowsy. Her eyelids began to droop heavily until she fell fast asleep, remembering no more of the eventful day until her mother's hands removing her boots woke her briefly, as she was laid down on the hard wooden squab.

# 3

# Scarlet Fever

Jim's father, Tom, was a spry old man and Nellie's memory retained a clear vision of him long after his death. He usually wore a cloth cap and rough jacket together with a pair of baggy corduroy trousers. He was quite a small man, although all four of his sons were well above six feet. He had fought through the Crimean War and his service to his country had resulted in the loss of an eye, which he covered with a black patch. Nellie recalled her uncles would pull his leg after hearing him recount some of his more hair-raising exploits. They would infuriate him by laughing and telling him 'Yo fought that war wi' sticks and bladders!'

Although the house in Station Street was tiny, consisting of two rooms up and down, Annie and Jim were happy to accommodate the old fellow. Indeed, Annie was often grateful for his presence as he would take the children off her hands when they were not at school. He took them for long leisurely walks to Bentley Common, or they would enjoy a visit to James Bridge Cemetery on a fine afternoon, wandering around the gravestones, Tom laboriously reading out the worn inscriptions for the children's edification.

One hot Sunday afternoon, soon after the street celebrations, they set out in the direction of Forge Lane. Stopping frequently to rest and enjoy the warm scented breeze, Nellie had loosed her grandad's hand and had wandered off alone to pick a few wild flowers for her mother. She knelt down on the rough verge near a clump of wild poppies and then quite suddenly she felt that it was too much trouble. Her head ached and she felt strangely wobbly. Dropping the few wilting flowers from her hot little hand, she rolled over and lay on her side, her head on a patch of dusty grass.

Tom and George soon became aware that Nellie was not trudging behind. With a cry of alarm, they looked back to see the tiny figure huddled by the roadside. George reached her first and was attempting to raise her to her feet when the old man came hurrying up. 'Out o' the way lad,' he panted 'let's see what's up wi' her.' He knelt down on trembling knees and peered anxiously out of his good eye at the flushed, tearful face of his granddaughter. 'There's summat the matter wi' her all right,' he announced. 'Her looks real poorly to me, we'd best get her back 'ome as quick as we can.'

Tom's wiry old arms still retained sufficient strength to lift the little girl and he hurried along as fast as he could go.

'Thee run on and tell thee feyther or thee mother George, and just be careful crossin' t'hoss road!'

Nellie lay whimpering in her grandfather's arms, hearing his hoarse laboured breath as he struggled up a sharp incline. All the time he kept talking to her, telling her she was his best little wench and she'd soon be better. He could have wept with relief at the sight of Annie and another woman approaching. George must have put every effort into his flight home.

The pressure on Tom's arms eased as Annie took the child from him. 'No need to kill yerself, dad,' she rebuked him. 'I dare say it's not that bad but Jim's gone for Dr Magrane.'

The neighbour, Mrs Lucas, peered at Nellie, lifting her clothes between grimy fingers. 'I can tell thee wot's the matter wi' her, Annie,' she announced. 'Her's got the scarlet fever!'

'Am yer sure?' cried Annie.

'As sure as I can be,' nodded her neighbour with just a hint of smug satisfaction. 'I've seen it before and yer know as the doctor won't let yer keep her at 'ome if he knows you've got a lad as well, it's infectionous yer see.'

When Nellie heard these words she immediately tightened her hands into a stranglehold round her mother's neck and broke into a loud wail. Annie struggled to loosen her grip. 'Now stoppit Nellie. Yer won't 'ave to goo anywhere if yer shut up.'

As the little procession approached Heath Road, Annie had decided what she must do. Before reaching the house she whispered a few words to George, who nodded his head and turned to trot back down the road, before disappearing into one of the long entries.

Dr Magrane was the parish doctor and had once been a naval surgeon. He visited his patients driven in a smart pony drawn trap by a man named Mr Ray, who looked after the pony and saw to the general upkeep of the trap. The doctor arrived at the house shortly after Nellie had been laid down and, bending over, he quickly confirmed Mrs Lucas' diagnosis.

'Are there any more children in this house?' he asked Annie.

'No, doctor,' she replied without hesitation.

'Good, good,' said Dr Magrane, 'in that case you can nurse her at home. I want you to go to the Town Hall first thing in the morning,' he continued. 'Ask for some disinfectant and you must be sure to use it everywhere and in all the washing. Call for me if you are worried and I would advise the other members of the family to sleep downstairs.' After a few more words of advice, the doctor left. Jim followed him to the door and when the trap had disappeared smartly round the corner, he turned to Annie and asked in some bewilderment 'Where's George and why did yer tell the doctor Nellie was the only one?'

'George is goin' ter stop wi' your Sarah for a bit, else Nellie would've 'ad ter go to the Fever Hospital and I can look after 'er just as well meself.'

Later, with Nellie tucked up in her tiny bedroom, two mattresses were hauled downstairs while Annie fixed a sheet over the doorway to Nellie's room. She would manage on a chair beside the bed for a few nights, she told herself. It would be better than traipsin' up and downstairs all night disturbing the men.

# 4

# Lil

Jim's dad had no permanent home of his own and would stay for a short time with each of his sons in turn. Within a few days of Nellie's illness, during which time he and Jim were confined to the ground floor, Tom decided it was time he was on the move.

'Yo cor hardly swing a cat round in 'ere,' he complained to Annie. 'I'd best goo and see our Sam for a bit. Yo' can shift one o' them mattresses back upstairs then.'

Annie was secretly relieved, although she would not have hurt the old man's feelings by letting him see. 'Please yerself, dad,' she said. 'We'll let yer know as soon as Nellie's better. I expect as Sam and Cal will be glad to see yer.'

Tom left later that morning after helping Annie upstairs with his mattress and getting together his few belongings. As soon as he had gone, Annie decided to give the room a really good clean as this had been almost impossible to do properly with the room being so small, normally slightly cluttered and then filled to capacity with the two mattresses.

She seized the remaining mattress and struggled to heave it into the backyard, to be followed immediately by two pegged rugs. After filling a chipped enamel bucket with hot water and soft brown soap, she fell to her knees and began to scrub the red quarry tiles. While the floor was drying, she went outside, took up one of the rugs and banged it hard against the wall, sending the dust flying in a choking cloud.

''Ow's your Nellie today, then?' croaked the husky voice of her next-door neighbour, who had appeared at her door upon hearing Annie's strenuous efforts outside.

'Oh her's a bit better.' coughed Annie, dust clogging her throat. 'I wish I could get 'er to stop scratchin' though. I've plastered 'er wi' calamine lotion but it don't seem ter do much good.'

Annie was reluctant to waste time talking today, although she was usually prepared for a good gossip when she had the time to spare.

'I thought I'd 'ave a good clean-up today,' she told her friend. 'Nellie's asleep, Jim's out of the road and his dad's gone to stop wi' Sam for a bit.'

'I thought as I 'adn't seen 'im about this mornin',' nodded Mrs Lucas. 'Still, it's less for you to do while Nellie's in bed.'

'I suppose so,' agreed Annie. 'Her's no trouble really but 'er 'as been that poorly that I've 'ad ter sit with 'er and I can't get out to the shops. I was wonderin' if you'd be gooin' up the town today?'

'I shall be later on, what dost want me to get?'

Annie considered, 'Well I could do with a loaf and I think I'll mek a stew for Jim's supper. He's werkin' late today. Could yer get me three pennorth o' bits and some onions. That'll do 'cos I've got some carrots and parsnips. I'll just slip in and get me purse.'

Annie hurried into the house, and emerged a moment later with a black oilcloth bag and a few coins. 'Thanks, Lizzie,' she smiled gratefully, as she handed them over the fence. 'It'll save me a fair bit o' time today and I can get me curtains washed as well, they could do with it.'

'See yer later then, Annie. Thee cost tell Nellie I might pop into Sleath's on me way back and get 'er a few sweets.' She disappeared into her house and Annie resumed her rug-beating.

Later that afternoon, Annie thankfully collapsed into a chair. A delicious stew bubbled merrily away on the hob, releasing a fragrant steam, which pervaded the whole of the little house. The room was fresh with soap and polish and the black-leaded grate shone like black satin, a token of Annie's hard work. The lace curtains billowed gently on the line, later to be draped at the spotless windows and Nellie slept aloft, much comforted by the pennorth of sweets purchased by the kindly Mrs Lucas.

Annie was tired out. She had slept little of late, anxiously watching over her little girl when her temperature had soared, as she tossed in a fever, crying out that her throat hurt and her head ached. Annie had patiently done everything she could to make Nellie more comfortable, dosing her and frequently sponging the hot little limbs. The red spots, which had first appeared on her chest, had rapidly spread over the rest of her body and her mother had to repeatedly try to restrain her from scratching. She was worn out too from the number of times she'd had to wash the bed-clothes when Nellie was sick.

The fever had subsided now but Annie was still hard put to it, to find sufficient clean cloths to stop the discharge from the child's ears, nose and throat. She had meticulously carried out the doctor's instructions and had disinfected everything that came into contact with the patient. Dr Magrane had impressed upon Annie that the child would be infectious for five to six weeks, and would require careful nursing and a long convalescence in order to avoid complications. Every day Jim called in at Sarah's to see George to make sure he was well. Annie was always relieved when he returned to report that the lad was 'bostin' with health and bein' spoiled rotten.'

A knock on the door woke Annie with a start.

'It's only me, Annie,' called the voice of her sister, Lil. She got to her feet, rubbing her eyes and stretching her arm to ease the cramp. 'Come on in, Lil, I must 'ave dropped off.' Lil put her shopping bag on the floor and sat down on the hard ladder-backed chair under the window. She looked hard at her sister, remarking, 'You'm lookin' a bit rough, Annie, I doe suppose you'm gerrin' much rest wi' Nellie. 'Ow is the little 'un today?'

'A bit better, Lil. At least her's managed to suck a few sweets Lizzie bought her, but I'll be glad when her can get a good meal down her, her looks nothin' but skin an' bone.'

'I shouldn't worry,' said Lil reassuringly, 'I expect as her'll pick up in a day or two, you just be thankful the t'other one's all right. I suppose he's enjoyin' himself at Sarah's aint 'e? Yo watch he woe want to come wum.'

Annie smiled in agreement and went out into the brewhouse to fill the kettle. After placing it on the fire to boil, she said 'I'll just pop up an' 'ave a look at 'er then we'll 'ave a cup of tea.'

''Ere, just a minute,' exclaimed Lil, rummaging through her shopping bag, 'I bought this for the little 'un.' She took out a coloured picture book and handed it to Annie. 'Oh, you shouldn't 'ave,' cried Annie gratefully. 'It must 'ave cost a fortune.'

'No it day,' replied Lil. 'I got it chep at the market.'

Lil lived in a small terraced house consisting of two up and two down in Snapes Yard near St Lawrence's Church and in it she had raised five children. Every Saturday morning she arose at 5.00 a.m. and in order to supplement her housekeeping money by a meagre five or six shillings, she would help to erect the trestles and stalls for the market which commenced at Lloyds Bank and ran along Church Street to the end of Bilston Street. The market sold everything from ribbons to chickens and flanked the horse road on either side. One of the most popular stalls, at least with the children, was the sweet stall which occupied a spot outside Salisbury's, the little old shop where a variety of sweets were made on the premises.

Although she began her working day virtually at the crack of dawn, it was often striking midnight by the church clock, when at last the heavy trestles had been dismantled for another week and Lil was able to fall wearily into her bed. When Nellie and George were older they would enjoy helping to light the gas flares, which cast a warm yellow glow into the darkening night and onto the faces of late shoppers hanging around hoping to pick up a bargain.

Long and hard Lil worked for what some might deem a small reward but she took great satisfaction in keeping her tiny house clean and neat and earning the extra shillings which enabled her children to attend school properly shod and warmly clothed. One unfortunate trait only Lil possessed; she was what was known as light-fingered and whenever she paid a visit to friends or relations she would take advantage of the temporary absence from the room of her hostess in order to purloin tea, sugar, salt or any other commodity easily transferable to one of her pockets. She stole nothing of real value but at a time when every copper counted, Lil's lapses, if discovered, were looked upon as unforgivable.

She busied herself in the scullery, bringing in two clean cups and the sugar and milk. She placed them on the table, the wood bleached almost white with the daily scrubbings and the grain standing out in hard ribs. Having washed the teapot in readiness, she reached down the tea caddy which stood on the mangle shelf. The shelf was Annie's pride. It had a red chenille mantle cloth with a fringe of gold bobbles and on it were placed a few of her most valued possessions, including a heavy wooden clock and two china dogs won for her by Jim at Darlaston Wake. Annie looked forward to the day when she could afford to buy a matching chenille table-cloth to cover her bare table. She felt it would help make the room a little more cosy. She was a born homemaker and took such a pride in keeping the house spotless. It was a pleasure rather than a chore to black-lead the fire grate each Friday morning and scrub her front doorstep before applying the red ochre. She made the most of every penny Jim gave her and the money stretched further than that of most of her neighbours. She also took pride in her appearance and, although her wardrobe tended to be rather skimpy, she would cover a much-worn dress with a spotless white apron and her dark hair was always neatly bundled on top of her head and firmly secured with steel pins.

She had little real claim to beauty but she had a pleasant face which, more often than not, wore a smile. At that time life had not begun to etch the lines of worry, grief and guilt, which would later appear and deepen with every passing year.

Annie descended the stairs and sat down, taking the steaming cup of tea Lil handed her.

'Ta, Lil. Nellie's pleased to death with the picture book. It ought to keep 'er 'appy for a bit.'

'Well, I only called in to see 'ow 'er was,' said Lil, supping her tea noisily. 'I can't stop long.'

''Ow's Jack?' asked Annie, 'is that cuff of 'is any better?'

'No,' sniffed Lil, 'and I cor gerrim to goo and see the doctor. I've towed 'im I'm gerrin' fed up of hearin' 'im hackin' away, but he's as stubborn as a bloody mule.'

'Ar, I know,' agreed Annie. 'Jim can be the same sometimes.'

'Ger away wi' yer, he's as daft as a bruch wi' you an' the little 'uns, 'e thinks as the sun shines out o' yer ear 'oles.'

Annie laughed, picking up the teapot. 'Do yer want another, Lil?'

'No ta, Annie.' Lil shook her head, getting stiffly to her feet. 'I'm off wum or the old man'll be wonderin' if he's gonna ger 'is tay tonight. I'm glad Nellie's on the mend, yo wants ter mek sure as yo get some rest or you'll be laid up next.'

Annie followed her sister to the door. 'Thanks again, Lil. I might pop in on Sat'day if I can ger up ter the market.' She watched and waved for a while before returning to the house.

# 5

# A Good Knees Up

Several people enquired after Nellie's health during the few weeks that followed. It was a time when a family's troubles were shared by relatives, friends and neighbours alike. When a woman was confined, neighbours living in the same party yard would each offer some kind of support, either looking after the children or getting the old man a meal. Help would be given with shopping and washing and, if necessary, food was shared. In times of trouble and bereavement a family would never have to cope alone with sorrow, for it would be truly shared by one and all.

Yard parties were a common feature of life when Nellie was young. A birthday party would be celebrated with everyone contributing some tasty morsel. Later on, when the kids were worn out with the day's revels and bellies were full to repletion, they would be sent up the 'wooden hill'. A barrel of beer would later be hoisted onto a wooden table brought out of somebody's kitchen, and neighbours would gather from nearby houses as word flew swiftly round that Mrs Whatsit at no. 28 was having a knees up.

If anyone owned a piano or harmonium it would be put to good use, as voices strengthened and refreshed by a few pints of best bitter were raised in unison with a rendition of a few of the good old songs. Very popular were 'Don't go down the Mine, Dad', 'Thora', 'Bank of England' and 'She was only a Bird in a Gilded Cage'. The revels would often continue far into the night until the last of the beer had been consumed. Friends would then bid each other a loud and oft-repeated 'Goo' night, goo' night, see thee termorra!' and stagger away happily to bed.

Annie particularly enjoyed these social occasions. She was at that time of a most cheerful disposition and loved a good laugh. It was a popular notion among the women in the street to take an evening trip to Kinver or Brewood in a hired brake, which set off from The Star Music Hall, a pub on the Walsall road. The only drawback, as

*The Elwells' home.*

far as Annie was concerned, was that these outings cost 1*s* and there were few of Annie's acquaintances who could readily find the cash.

The idea came to her when she was halfway through Old Knowley's washing. In order to add a little extra to the family income, Annie took in the washing of Mr and Mrs Knowles – Mr Knowles being commonly known to all as Old Knowley. An aunt of Annie's named Sarah Steadman lived in the same yard and she washed for Mr and Mrs Elwell on the Walsall road. It occurred to Annie that if one of the bundles of washing was pawned, it would provide sufficient money to pay for an evening's outing. Accordingly, it became a regular practice that on the day of the trip Old Knowley's washing would be taken, minus two pinafores to the pawnshop. Later that evening Aunt Sarah and Annie would set forth attired in the same freshly washed and starched pinafores to enjoy an evening's excursion. The following day Aunt Sarah's washing would be dispatched to the pawnshop in order to redeem Old Knowley's bundle. This little arrangement continued for some time, undetected by the two owners of the much-travelled washing and greatly enjoyed by Jim and others who were privy to it.

*James
Bridge
Cemetery.*

As the years passed, the first lines of grief were engraved upon Annie's face. Her third child was christened Elizabeth Nancy, and known throughout her brief existence as Lizzie. Two years and two months after her birth, the little girl died of measles, in spite of Annie's devoted nursing. The tiny coffin was laid to rest in James Bridge Cemetery, Annie insisting that her baby lie in its own grave, as it was customary for an infant's coffin to occupy that of an adult.

As time passed other babies were born and in almost regular spaces of eighteen months after the death of Lizzie, first Evelyn, then Tom, named for his grandfather, were born. Grandad Tom still came to stay with the family and one of Nellie's clearest memories was of one Sunday evening setting out for a walk with grandad pushing young Tom in his pushchair with George on one side and Nellie on the other.

It had been a glorious summer day, the late evening air still warm and fragrant as they trudged along Forge Lane. Through the cornfields astir in a gentle breeze and studded with bright scarlet poppies they went. In the distance they could hear the church bells of St Paul's and by way of accompaniment, the old pushchair went squeaking along. Ever afterwards, to the time when Nellie grew old, the sound of a child's squeaking pram or pushchair immediately brought to her mind that walk with her young brothers and her grandad, as fresh as though it had been yesterday. She remembered the old man breaking into song and urging them to join in. The children knew most of the old songs by heart as it was a regular habit for uncles and aunts to visit on Saturday nights. The evening would almost certainly end with a sing-song and Nellie would listen carefully to the words and soon be joining in, adding her clear, young voice to theirs.

# 6

# A Plot is Hatched

Jim Askey was a popular man, known to his friends as 'Buller'. He was hardworking, honest, with a respect for women and regard for his fellow man. His cheerful demeanour and open-handed generosity earned him many friends. Also, his capacity for the local brew and an ability to use his fists with devastating effect when necessary, was much admired.

His only real fear in life was that there might come a time when he would be unable, through illness or lack of work, to provide for his family. At a time when real prosperity belonged to those few of Jim's acquaintance, who could afford to live in posh houses, wear expensive clothes and whose children could eat what they fancied even though they weren't hungry, Jim and most of the families he knew well were contented if they could afford to pay the rent, have one good meal a day and count on regular employment. It was so often necessary, as with Annie, for the women to take on extra work, washing and cleaning for those who could afford to pay. In times of real hardship there was always the pawnshop just off the Walsall road and it was not considered shameful to be a regular patron of that establishment. In spite of the lack of financial security, the little back-to-back houses bred folk who, as well as having a close acquaintance with hunger and worry, seemed embued with an ability to live life in the true meaning of neighbourliness and friendship. They took each day as it occurred and made their own enjoyment. Women with scant means learned well how to grapple with dirt and disease. The kids often went out to play without a behind in their trousers and wore holes in their boots, but still they retained a good measure of happiness, displayed great inventiveness in their games and had a healthy respect for their parents. The men-folk would hand over whatever amount they considered sufficient for their families' weekly requirements, and then retire to the bar of their favourite local and pour what remained down their throats.

Jim sat in his usual corner of The Vine supping his beer. His only companion at that moment was Elijah Brown, the same proud father, whose thunder Jim had stolen some years before. It had taken a long time for 'Lijah to forgive the slight to his puny baby but he and Jim sat together now amicably enough. 'Lijah was inclined to a certain dourness of character and was not much sought after as a companion and he secretly envied Jim his popularity. His wife was reputed to be a woman of many words and most of these sharpened to a fine cutting edge found a frequent target in her unhappy husband. He sought regular solace and refuge at The Vine where he said little but observed much. After taking a long pull at his beer, he turned and looked at Jim.

'I sin yer owd man up Bentley Common last Sundy.'

'Oh ar,' replied Jim 'he usually teks our Tum fer a walk on Sundy mornin's.'

'I know 'e does,' nodded 'Lijah, 'I sin 'im theer a few times.'

'Oh ar,' repeated Jim wondering what 'Lijah was getting at.

'Every time I sin im 'e's sittin' under t'edge fast asleep. I reckon anybody could cum an tek off wi' yower babby. Serve 'im bloody right as well!'

Jim's immediate reaction was one of concern but after a moment's thought, an idea occurred to him which brought a gleam of amusement to his eye. It was Saturday and one or two of his brothers would be dropping in that evening for the usual get-together and bite of supper. Jim would put to them his plan which should provide a bit of fun and at the same time teach the old fellow a lesson.

Nellie looked forward to Saturday nights and the company of her relatives. She was particularly fond of her Uncle Joe, who was a good deal like her dad, not only in appearance but also the way in which he teased her gently. Nellie was rather a solemn child, given to taking life very seriously and worrying about things rather more than was necessary. However, in the right company she would blossom and respond readily to the little jokes directed at her. The only teasing Nellie wouldn't tolerate was from a pal of Jim's called Buzzer. He would take hold of the legs of her bloomers and hitch them up as high as they would go. Her little legs would dance up and down in rage as she would scream in protest until her mother laughingly intervened.

Nellie sat on the wooden squab, that item of furniture common to most households. It was the name given to a type of settle with high back and sides made more comfortable with a small mattress seat which was usually covered with brightly patterned material. Uncle Sam sat on one side of her with Aunt Cal on the other. Cal was a little woman, rather on the skinny side and had an almost hatchet-sharp face. Her thin sandy hair was scraped back tightly behind her ears and secured into a bun with steel pins. In addition to her rather forbidding appearance, Cal had a somewhat caustic wit and a tendency to speak her mind, but she enlivened any company and was reasonably well-liked. Annie busied herself with the teapot as Jim brought in more coal to replenish the fire, for the evening was turning chilly. George sat on the rag hearth rug, hands clasping his knees as he stared dreamily into the dancing flames. Everybody looked up as the door was briefly knocked and opened to reveal Uncle Joe, followed by his wife, Ethel. The room seemed at once to explode into life. Ethel was a large woman, much given to loud conversation and hearty laughter. Her eyes, when she laughed, would almost disappear into her flesh and her chins would ripple and wobble like jelly. The children adored her and she was often the confidante they sought with their little troubles. Cal sometimes disapproved of her immense sister-in-law's easy going, slightly slap-dash administrations to her husband and family and was often provoked into giving Ethel the benefit of her unwelcome advice.

Ethel settled her bulk comfortably into the only chair in the house capable of withstanding the strain, with much puffing and blowing, while Joe slipped into the place which Nellie had just vacated. Cal observed the efforts of Ethel to regain control of her breath, then remarked 'Bloody 'ell, Ethel you've only 'ad to walk hop, skip an' a jump an' look 'ow breathless you bin. Why doe yer try an'gerra bit o' weight off?' Turning to Joe she continued, 'You ought to get 'er to do summat abowt it, it's doin' her no good, all that fat!'

Joe chuckled, 'I reckon as it's a bit too late to do anythin' Cal, her's always bin sort of on the plump side.' Cal snorted, 'Plump! More like the side of a bloody 'ouse an' I swear as her gets bigger every time I see 'er.'

This reference to her size did not upset Ethel in the least, and she collapsed into soundless laughter, but Annie was a little embarrassed by Cal's outspokenness and hastily suggested that they might all like a cup of tea. As the cups were passed round, the women settled themselves comfortably for a lively gossip. This was tempered, however, with discretion, as the children were present and was merely an exchange of news of their doings and the more innocent ones of their neighbours since they last met. George was more interested anyway in the men's talk of pigeon-flying or a description of the latest fight to have taken place on top of the Black Nob.

It had been a mystery for some time among the women of James Bridge as to why their men-folk would disappear in the early hours of Sunday morning, explaining, if discovered, that they were just going for a walk.

The solution was found when Cal and one or two others stealthily left their houses shortly after their husbands had departed, and followed them along Station Street. Up they climbed to the top of a high bank known as the Black Nob. Gathered at the top were small groups of men milling around and obviously waiting for some action to begin. At a signal, two men stripped off their jackets and assumed a fighting stance. A bare-fisted fight then ensued with a great deal of noisy encouragement from the onlookers. As Cal and the other women were the only females present, once they had witnessed the beginning of the proceedings, they decided it would be as well to retire unobserved. These regular bouts of fisticuffs were the result of disagreements and arguments begun in the pub the night before. As neither of the antagonists would then be in a fit state to settle things at that moment, a confrontation would be arranged for the following morning, when honour would be satisfied.

Nellie squatted on a small wooden stool at Aunt Ethel's knee. She was content to let the buzz of conversation wash over her head as her mind grew preoccupied with little thoughts of her own. She was now six years old and had attended Salisbury Street School for the last twelve months, displaying a child's uncomplaining acceptance of the conditions which prevailed in the classroom at that time. Discipline was rigid. Almost the whole of the timetable was devoted to learning the three Rs, with very little of the modern school's wide variety of subjects, some intended for the child's enjoyment as well as its academic advancement. Nellie had made a few friends at school, the closest of these and her most constant playmate was a child called Edie Clamp. Edie was a little older than Nellie and had already been attending school for some months prior to Nellie's debut. She had taken the frightened little girl under her wing and had greatly eased her entry into the ways of the new school. They shared all their small joys and grievances and much of their free time was spent together. Nellie's hand crept to the little pocket in the folds of her dress, and as her fingers made contact with a hard sticky substance she smiled to herself. They were still there, the two sugar fish she had saved, intending to eat one herself tomorrow and save the other for Edie's delectation. She sighed. It had been a lovely day. Saturday was probably her favourite day of the week. Each Saturday dinnertime, when Jim returned, his children would be waiting to meet him. He would stoop down and swing young Tom onto his shoulders and with the others trailing beside him they would make their way over Bull Piece and up to the Penny Bazaar in King Street, so named because nothing cost more than a penny. Nellie's final choice today had been a little green cardboard purse with an elastic band to secure the flap. Evelyn had selected a minute doll's pram, while George, faced with a decision between a catapult and a whip and top, had tried Jim's patience by his dithering about, until his father had forced him to pick up the catapult with the threat that 'he would get nothin' if he day 'urry up an' mek 'is mind up.' Tom was happy with a picture book. Then, with everyone satisfied, they made their way to Lewis's sweet shop. Here Jim made no attempt to rush them, the choice of sweets being a most important decision to make. Nellie's current favourite were the sugar fish, but she peered anxiously over the vast selection, her hand hovering over one and then another before finally deciding on the fish once more. The next and final visit was to Fortnam's greengrocer's shop where Jim purchased a few grapes for Annie, who had a great fondness for them.

Nellie was brought back to the present by the sudden scrape of chairs on the quarry tiles and the departure of the men-folk. This followed the usual Saturday night routine, whereby Jim and his brothers would adjourn to the pub to sup a swift pint before returning with the large china jug borrowed from upstairs, brimming with beer. In their absence, Annie would prepare a simple supper consisting usually of bread and cheese with pickles and enlivened with a tasty hunk of pig's pudding. She moved about the room, opening a cupboard high up to the left of the fireplace. Taking down half a dozen white plates decorated with a delicate pale pink flower pattern, she dusted them lovingly with a clean cloth. She liked to keep these best plates just for high days and holidays, but she was obliged to use them now, owing to an unfortunate accident which had put paid to most of her everyday plates. She intended to replace these with a few cheap ones from the market as soon as she could. In the meantime, she handled her plates with care, keeping a watchful eye on their usage.

While Ethel chatted to the children, Cal helped Annie with the preparations for supper and the washing up of the used cups, and, when everything was ready, they sat down to await their husbands' return.

George was asking Ethel, 'Am you gonna sing tonight, Aunty?' for in spite of her bulk and shortage of breath following any physical exertion, Ethel possessed a very fine singing voice, but was sometimes a little reluctant to perform.

'Oh, I doe now cock,' chuckled Ethel. 'I've got me new stays on t'night an' they doe arf pinch. I aint broke 'em in yet.'

'Why doe yer tek 'em off then,' suggested Annie, 'an' let yerself spread.'

'Lord, if 'er does that we woe be able to get 'er out o' the cheer,' said Cal.

'Goo on Aunty Ethel,' pleaded Nellie, 'sing me favourite please.'

'Oh, no,' protested George, 'if her sings that un you'll all be cryin' yer eyes out!'

Nellie's favourite was 'The Bank of England', a heartrending tale of a poor little boy, who desires to find the bank in order to carry a little gold home to his starving mother. The song ends when the child is run over by a carriage and with his last breath he implores:

> Where is the Bank of England,
> The place where they keep all the gold?
> Mother and brother are both so ill,
> Hungry and cold.
> I've never seen any gold in my life,
> It's a beautiful thing I am told,
> Perhaps t'would cure brother and cheer up my mother,
> If I bought them a ha-porth of gold.

These words, rendered by Ethel in the most feeling way, were enough to touch the hardest heart and always provoked tears from the females in the company, who joined in the final chorus, emitting many a loud sniff. Many of the songs popular when Nellie was young had a sad theme and were always performed with utmost pathos. It was quite easy in those days to relate to the poor old couple whose home and possessions are sold as they are forced to go 'over the hill' (to the workhouse) to live out their few remaining days in cruel separation, torn from their life's partner.

There were the songs telling of poor little barefoot children, living in poverty and squalor, with their mother, toiling day in and day out in an effort to keep her family alive, while her drunken brute of a husband gives no thought to his family's welfare. This, of course, was a picture of the darkest side of existence and the lives of those who sang of these unfortunates seemed joyous indeed by comparison, which is probably why the songs were so much appreciated and relished.

The kettle was just coming to the boil, when loud shouts of laughter were heard outside.

''Ark at them buggers,' cried Cal, 'I bet they've 'ad more than one!'

'I 'eard that m'gel,' said Jim, grabbing Cal by the waist and swinging her off her feet. 'Put me down you big fool,' cried Cal. 'You'll knock Annie's plates off the table.' Jim released her with a laugh and pulled Nellie's hair. 'Well, if yo ay 'ad more than one, what you actin' like that for?' sniffed Cal, who disapproved of any display of high spirits.

'It's just summat as we've bin thinkin' on', said Jim winking at his brothers. 'We've just fixed up a little joke to play on feyther tomorrow.'

'Oh no, Jim,' protested Annie. 'It's a shame the way you treat that poor old chap, you'm always pullin' 'is leg. And you two am just as bad as 'im,' she said severely glaring at the two grinning faces of his brothers.

'Well, let's 'ave some grub me wench, an' I'll tell thee all about it.'

Chairs were hitched up to the table and thick slices of bread and butter distributed together with generous wedges of cheese. A big jar of onions of Annie's own pickling stood in the centre of the table was attacked with much frequency by all. After he had taken the edge off his appetite, Jim began by telling them of his conversation with Elijah Brown in The Vine.

Annie was filled with indignation, when she heard how Jim's father would fall asleep, leaving her precious Tom unsupervised while he pursued his slumbers. Jim laid his hand soothingly on her arm while he unfolded his plan to teach the old fellow a lesson. Ethel had just taken a gigantic swallow of bread and cheese, when she went off into a paroxysm of gasps and undulations. Joe stood up and smote her a mighty blow on the back.

'Oh, dear,' she gasped, 'Oh, Jim, you'll be the death o' me,' she cried wiping her eyes on the back of her hand. 'You' – her next words were stifled in a sudden fit of coughing. She heaved and struggled for breath as her face took on a purple hue. Joe repeated the blows with the flat of his hand upon Ethel's ample back. After nearly five minutes had elapsed, to the consternation of everybody, Ethel was sufficiently recovered to explain that 'a crumb must 'ave gone down the wrong way.'

When the panic had subsided, everyone began to laugh, even Cal's tough old face creased into a rusty smile as she gave her opinion. 'Serve the owd bugger right, let's 'ope as it'll learn 'im in future. That is,' she remarked with a glance at Annie 'if you'm gonna trust 'im again with your Tum.'

'Oh, yes,' cried Annie. 'It 'ud break 'is heart if I day let 'im 'ave the kids, he's bin golden to 'em. An' as for you two,' she spoke sharply to Nellie and George, who were still giggling, 'Doe you dare say a word ter ya grandad in the mornin' or you'll both gerra good thrairpin.'

The evening continued on a jolly note and when the remains of the meal had been cleared away and Annie's precious plates restored to the safety of the cupboard, Ethel, as Nellie had hoped, was persuaded to give a rendition of 'The Bank of England'.

'Lovely,' sighed Nellie, as the final notes quivered and faded. Annie dabbed her eyes and nodded in agreement while Cal, having forgotten to bring a handkerchief, applied the edge of her 'pinner' to her somewhat moist red nose.

The men, too, were most appreciative of Ethel's efforts, but decided that it was time to introduce a lighter note into the proceedings. 'Otherwise,' said Jim, 'we shall all get melancholy.' Sam volunteered to restore an atmosphere of cheerfulness with a lively interpretation of 'She was only a Bird in a Gilded Cage'.

In spite of the lack of musical accompaniment, a harmonium being rather low on Annie's list of priorities, the entertainment lacked nothing in the enthusiasm, either on the part of the performer or in the appreciation of his audience.

At ten o'clock Nellie yawned hugely and was immediately pounced upon by her mother. 'Off yer goo, up the wooden hill. It's way past yer bed time. And you!' she said, waving a hand towards George in a gesture of dismissal.

They both knew it was no use appealing to Jim for an extension for they had already exceeded their usual bedtime, even for a Saturday night. After wishing everyone goodnight George paused at the stairs. 'Dad,' he asked pleadingly, 'can I goo wi' yer termorrow?'

'I doe think soo lad,' replied Jim. 'I 'ates ter think what yer grandad's language'll be like, but I'll tell thee all about it when we gets wum.' Amid their laughter, George reluctantly followed his sister upstairs.

At about a quarter to twelve Cal and Ethel decided it was time to depart. 'I've enjoyed me supper Annie,' Ethel wheezed. 'It were a nice bit o' cheese that.' 'Ar,' agreed Joe, 'went down a treat wi' a good drap o' beer. I'll see thee termorra then, Jim. What time dist say the owd 'un comes ter fetch the babby?'

'About half past ten, but we'd best mek sure an' gi' 'im plenty o' time afore we gets theer.'

As Joe lived in Station Street too, next to The Vine, and Sam lived just a few houses away in Heath Road, it was arranged that the brothers would meet on the corner of The Vine at half past eleven the next morning.

Goodnights having been said and the visitors having departed, Jim locked the door and banked up the fire before finally winding the clock on the mantelshelf. Annie's last task upon retiring for the night was to open the oven door in the firegrate and give a stir to the rabbit and shin, cooking in the stew jar. This, eaten with hunks of bread, would serve for the family's Sunday breakfast and would be done to perfection when Annie and Jim arose. It was the custom on Sunday mornings for the children to remain in bed, regardless of whatever early hour they may have awakened, until their parents had eaten.

'That smells good, Annie,' sniffed Jim appreciatively as the oven door was opened, 'although I couldn't manage any just now.'

'I doe expect as you could on top of a belly full o' beer,' snapped Annie.

'What's up wi' you then?' asked Jim, surprised by the sharp tone of her voice.

'Oh nuthin. I'm just wonderin' if you ought ter play that silly trick on yer feyther, that's all. He aint gonna like it, yer know.'

'I doe suppose as you'd like it neither,' Jim retorted, 'if somethin' was to 'appen to our Tum. It aint just a joke yer know. If he's gonna tek the kids out then he must look after 'em prop'ly. I know as 'Lijah Brown's a troublemekka but 'e's right yer know, somebody might easy come by an' tek the babby off while the owd mon's asleep.'

'Oh, I suppose so,' sighed Annie 'any road, I'm off ter bed. Doe forget to turn the lamp out an' mind yer doe wake the little 'uns when yer come up.'

# 7

# A Lesson Learned

Jim's father was lodging with another of his sons, also called Tom, who lived at the Pleck in Walsall. Having caught a tram to James Bridge the next morning, he arrived in good time to collect his young grandson for their Sunday morning walk. Annie opened the door to him with some misgivings. 'Come on in, Dad' she smiled.

Jim sat in the corner polishing his best boots. 'Mornin' dad!' he greeted the old man cheerfully. Tom sat down on the squab, unwound his white muffler and removed his cap, 'How do' he replied, nodding to Annie. He looked around the room 'Wheer's the kids then,' he asked.

'Oh, they've gone to hear Mr Jordan, they'll be back in a minute,' replied Annie. Tom nodded, remembering that on Sunday mornings, Mr Jordan, who lived a few houses away, always opened his front door on fine mornings to play hymns on the organ for the enjoyment of those who appreciated his music. There were usually a number of children thronged around his doorway but it must be admitted that the greater attraction for them were the small cakes freshly baked by Mrs Jordan which she freely distributed amongst them.

'George 'as got Tom all ready in the pushcheer,' Annie told him, 'do yer want a cuppa tea while you'm waitin' or do yer want ter fetch 'im now?'

'I may as well 'ave a cup, ta Annie,' answered Tom. 'I sin all the kids outside Jordan's but I day notice owern amongst 'em.' Jim was tempted to make a joke about his father's eyesight, but thought better of it. Instead he enquired after the old man's health and asked how long he intended to stay with Tom. 'I'm orlright wheer I bin at the present,' said his father. 'There's some decent pubs round theer an' I like a walk round Walsall market now an' agen.'

'Well you know you'm alwis welcome 'ere dad, whenever you'm ready,' put in Annie warmly. 'The kids love to 'ave you an' we miss yer Sat'day nights. Sam an' Joe was round last night an' we was just talkin' about you.' She stopped and caught Jim's grin. 'I mean ter say, they was askin' if we'd sin yer in the week,' she amended hurriedly.

'I might call in an' see 'em when we gets back from Bentley,' said Tom, sipping his tea after stirring it vigorously and blowing hard. Annie and Jim exchanged significant glances, he'd be seeing them sooner than he'd expected.

'Oh, well, I think I'll 'ave a stroll up and fetch Tum,' said the old man getting to his feet. He placed his empty cup on the table, wrapped his scarf once more around his neck and slapped his cap a couple of times on his corduroy trousers before placing it carefully on his head. Annie got up and followed him to the door. 'See yer later, dad. Oh, wait a bit. Tek this clean hankychief for Tom. He might need 'is nose wiping.' She opened the cupboard drawer and took out a red spotted hanky. 'Theer you am,' she said, tucking it into his trouser pocket. 'What a fuss', he sighed, 'he can use the back of his hand, can't he, same as me.'

'Go on,' laughed Annie. 'You'll 'ave 'im spittin' in t'hoss road next.'

'Ta-ra' called Jim, 'mind ow yer goo. I'll see ya later.'

'Oh, dad,' called Annie, darting after him. 'Tell George an' Nellie ter come an' get ready to goo to Aunt Nancy's!'

Tom waved an arm in response and continued on his way.

When Nellie and George returned with Evelyn they were smartened up by Annie before setting off on their usual Sunday visit to Jim's Aunt Nancy. Nancy and Alec Greenaway lived in a small house on the Walsall road near to the Star Music Hall, a local pub. The house was situated directly onto the main road, but the back garden, more frequently used by the children as access, was a riot of old-fashioned flowers. A dirt path edged with bricks led to the back door and on either side grew great masses of lupins, golden rod, roses and hollyhocks, blooming in summer in unhindered splendour, making the air heady with fragrance. Creeping ivy clung to the walls of the house, sending out tendrils in every direction. It grew so thickly round the door and windows that the room inside was permanently darkened. The back door stood open to the light warm breezes as the children entered the room, peering into the murky depths. When their eyes became adjusted to the gloom after the brilliance outside, they saw Aunt Nancy sitting as usual in her favourite rocking chair, placidly rocking backwards and forwards while her fingers flew in and out with a crochet hook into the latest piece of fancy work. She wore her Sunday best black dress with leg of mutton sleeves under a snowy pinafore. Her upswept hair revealed earrings of black jet and she wore long beads of the same stones around her neck. Nancy Greenaway had gained something of a reputation among the local population with a preparation called Baker's Drawing Ointment. She prepared the ointment herself from an old family recipe and it was sold for a few pence in small round boxes. Folks would come for miles around to buy it and they swore to the effectiveness of its healing properties when applied to all manner of skin ailments.

When greetings had been exchanged, the children arranged themselves on the black horsehair sofa, toes in position.

Nellie disliked these duty visits, when she was expected to sit quietly for the required length of time and not fidget, not an easy thing to do as the horsehair pricked the backs of tender young legs. The room was very quiet, the silence broken only by the ponderous tick of the ancient grandfather clock in the corner and the frantic buzzing of a large meat fly trapped against the window pane. There was, however, plenty to engage her interest as Nellie's eyes travelled slowly round the room. Aunt Nancy had a great fondness for china ornaments and, over the years, she had amassed quite a collection. There was a large oil painting hanging over the mantelshelf and Nellie never wearied of looking at it. It was a forest scene with mysterious depths and many coloured birds. To a child born and raised in dusty back streets, it seemed to satisfy some unspoken longing in her. After a time, Nellie's eyes moved on again to fasten upon various objects about the room. The round table with its red chenille cloth and a brass oil lamp with its painted shade, standing in the centre. A great carved over-mantel with its mirror over the fireplace reflected half a dozen of Aunt Nancy's most treasured china pieces.

A sharp dig in her side reminded Nellie that, in her brother's opinion, it was high time they were leaving.

Throughout their visit, Aunt Nancy's chair had continued its steady creak and her fingers had not paused in their labour, but her sharp eyes had observed George's action and the children's restlessness so she laid aside her work and the chair came to rest.

Interpreting this as the signal to leave, the children rose with relief and moving towards the door, blinked their eyes like little owls, as they left the room and stepped into the brilliant sunlight. Aunt Nancy followed them down the path and kissed each child before returning to the darkened silence of the house.

After collecting his grandson, Tom turned his footsteps in the direction of the Walsall road. Then, turning off left at the cemetery, he continued to push young Tom along the lane which passed beneath the Two Arches. It was a delightful morning in early May with the sun strengthening daily and the trees clothed in tender young green. The air was murmurous with the sound of insects and heavy with the scent of wild flowers. Tom slipped his hand inside his jacket pocket and he smiled contentedly as his fingers patted the bottle which reposed there. He gazed down affectionately on the head of the small boy, who was banging his heels against the footrest of the pushchair, in time with his tuneless crooning.

'I doe know what thee bist singin', lad,' remarked his grandad, 'but I reckon as I'll 'ave to learn thee a few good 'uns when theest a bit owder.'

*The Two Arches.*

They continued on their way, the old man greeting a few acquaintances, who were out to enjoy their usual Sunday morning constitutional. At the top of Bentley Mill Lane they turned off to the left along a narrow road. On the opposite side stretched Bentley Common, a vast sandy, hilly area, thickly dotted with gorse bushes and, on this particularly fine morning, a number of fathers with their youngsters, keeping them 'out o' the road for a bit,' while the wife got on with the preparations for the Sunday dinner.

It was too noisy however for Tom's liking; he avoided the common, sticking to the road until he arrived at his favourite spot. ''Ere we am young 'un,' he said, pulling the pushchair under the hedge as far as it would go. He sat down on the grass beside it and settled himself comfortably before withdrawing his bottle. Unscrewing the top, he tipped it up and took a long pull, gulping noisily and smacking his lips with appreciation. He wiped his mouth on the back of his hand, then became aware of his small grandson's fixed gaze. 'Bist thirsty chap? Here yo am. Yo can 'ave a quick swig but doe tell yer mother!' Young Tom transferred his eyes to the proffered bottle and he made a quick grab. 'Hey up, yer little bugger,' cried the old man rescuing his bottle before the lad could take more than a quick swallow. He chuckled as the youngster pulled a face. 'What's up Tom, doe yer like it then? Well I expect as you'll change yer mind when you'm a bit owder.'

When the bottle had been emptied and slung over the hedge, the old man settled himself again with his back resting comfortably against the thick supporting hedge. Before long his head had dropped forward onto his chest and the first loud snores shattered the silence of the morning. He had been sleeping peacefully for about half an hour when Jim, Joe and Sam furtively approached. Jim grabbed the pushchair swiftly before its young occupant had time to utter a cry of greeting upon seeing his father. The conspirators moved quickly and quietly to a place of concealment behind the hedge. They remained there for twenty minutes or so, stifling their laughter as the sounds of assorted snores and whistles reverberated on the air. 'I wonder 'ow long he's gonna kip for,' whispered Joe. 'All bloody day by the looks on it,' muttered Sam.

'Let's chuck a bibble at 'im,' suggested Jim. 'We can't wait round here all mornin'.'

This appealed to the others and they began to hunt around for suitable missiles. The second shot to be fired must have found its

*Joe and Sam, in the middle of the second row.*

unseen target, as the snores stopped suddenly to be followed by a series of bewildered grunts and then silence. All at once a piercing shriek rent the air. 'Oh my God, somebody's pinched the babby. Oh my God her'll bloody kill me, oh my God what shall I do?' The brothers clutched each other convulsed with silent laughter, as the air on the other side of the hedge began to turn blue. They fell about clapping hands over mouths to stifle their glee.

Gradually the swearing gave way to utterances of such despair and anguish that the men quickly sobered up and decided to make their presence known.

They discovered the old man running frantically up and down, pulling his hair. The look of relief on his face, when he caught sight of Tom safely strapped in his pushchair, at once brought a feeling of shame to his sons. As explanations were given, the old man's face grew black with rage, he almost danced in his anger and it was feared that he might have a seizure.

'Calm down, old fellow,' said Jim mildly. 'It were only meant as a joke.'

'A joke, a bloody joke!' shouted his father.

'Well, yer shouldn't 'ave gone ter sleep,' reasoned Jim. 'It could a bin somebody else as took 'im.'

When Tom had eventually calmed down, he admitted that maybe he did rest his eye for a few minutes. 'But that's all,' he protested. 'I never went right off.' His sons exchanged grins, remembering the shattering snores.

The tale was, of course, added to the family collection, to be taken out and given an airing at the Saturday night get-togethers. Nellie heard it laughed over often in later years, long after her grandad's death.

Another favourite story was told of how walnut shells were tied to the cat's feet and it was let loose to run over the bare floorboards of a room over that in which the old man was sleeping. He awoke in alarm upon hearing the pitter-patter overhead and yelled that the house must be haunted.

Jim would also recall how one Sunday morning when Annie, having taken George and Nellie to visit her father at Nottingham for the day, left his youngest sister, Nancy Leah, to supervise his midday meal. After taking his Sunday morning walk to Bentley, Jim returned home, looking forward to a basinful of cow's cheek with leeks. The house was empty when he arrived but a delicious smell filled the room. Smiling in anticipation, Jim lifted the lid of the stewjar, to be confronted by the large accusing eye of the unfortunate cow, Nancy Leah having neglected to remove it, either through ignorance or revulsion.

Annie would sometimes talk to the children of the time before she and Jim were married and he was employed on the construction of the new Darlaston Police Station in 1898. The day came when the work was finally completed and the gang of men knocked off around 12.30 p.m. Jim and his workmates decided to celebrate with a few pints at The Pretty Bricks. By 1.30 p.m. or thereabouts, the gang was roaring drunk. Jim could never remember afterwards who actually started the fight or how it happened that the police inspector and his sergeant appeared so promptly upon the scene, but it was apparent that he did not intend to go quietly. As the inspector advanced with his handcuffs at the ready, Jim felled him with a blow. He was eventually restrained however, the handcuffs were snapped on and he was hauled off to become the first occupant of the cells he had just finished building, less than two hours before. When requested to give his name, Jim was uncooperative. 'Same as me feyther's,' he replied.

'Well, what's his name then?' asked the constable with pen poised. 'Same as mine' answered Jim.

Still handcuffed, he was deposited into one of the new cells, the plaster barely dry. Left to himself Jim quickly sobered up, realising the enormity of his action in striking a police inspector in the performance of his duty. Rather than spend the night in the cell and then have to face the consequences, he decided to take matters into his own hands. Having noticed a hard wooden ledge which ran along the width of the cell, he knelt down and banged his head repeatedly on its sharp edge. As soon as he felt the warm trickle run down his nose and over his lips and had tasted the salty blood, he stood up, kicked on the cell door and yelled for the officer. 'What the bloody 'ell you bin doin' mate?' exclaimed the copper upon seeing Jim's battered visage.

Jim then explained earnestly that unless he was released into the bosom of his family without delay, he would be forced to make a report as to how he had been beaten up upon his arrest.

This outrageous bit of blackmail evidently had the desired effect and Jim was released forthwith.

# 8

# School Days

Nellie was seven when the family moved to no. 41 Tilley Street. Moving house was a comparatively simple and straightforward matter then. There was no shortage of empty dwellings and when Annie was told about the house by one of her neighbours, all she had to do after inspecting the outside and peering through the dirty curtainless windows was to go to 'Tight' Low's butcher's shop in High Street and collect the keys.

Tilley Street was only a short distance away from Station Street so a handcart hired from Charlie Simmonds, a local coal merchant, for 6*d* sufficed to carry the family's furniture and household effects in a few trips. There were four houses on either side of the long entry and no. 41 was the first one on the right. The party yard at the rear contained four brewhouses, one to be shared by two families. Behind the brewhouses was an area where the children were able to play. None of the houses had a garden. The strips between the back door and the brewhouses were laid with blue bricks and the remainder of the yard consisted of hard-packed earth. A high brick wall enclosed the rear of the yard behind which ran Gladstone Street.

The house was small. Upon entering the back door, the stairs went off immediately to the left. Next to the stairs door was a door leading down to the cellar. The living room was cosy, with a corner fireplace of black-lead and Annie placed her square wooden table underneath the window, which was immediately next to the back door. Against the opposite wall to the cellar and stairs stood a hard, one-sided sofa of black imitation leather, which she had bought to replace the old wooden squab. This, together with one or two odd chairs, completed the furnishings for the family's comfort.

The front room was of similar size but was rarely used. It had a small black firegrate, a table in the centre covered by a pretty tapestry cloth and along one wall stood a large chest of drawers. There was no door at the top of the box stairs and they led directly into the bedroom. From this main bedroom, a door opened into a smaller room beyond. In spite of these somewhat cramped conditions, the house was homely and cosy and the family soon settled in comfortably. Nellie grew very fond of the little house in Tilley Street and many years later when it stood forlornly empty, awaiting demolition, she would peep in sadly through the window, remembering it as it once was.

It was just after the move that events began to alter the pattern of Nellie's life. The saddest of these was the death of her grandfather. Tom was greatly missed by all who knew him and Annie and the family grieved for the old man.

Nellie left Salisbury Street School to attend the Central School in Slater Street. She remembered that on the last Friday afternoon at Salisbury Street, she and all her classmates were told to form a long crocodile. With their teacher in attendance they were taken to the new school and shown around their new classroom. The headmistress was named Miss Perks and Nellie's teacher was Miss Blewitt, later to become Mrs Perry.

Tom was causing his mother some annoyance at this time and she was fast losing patience with him. 'I doe like that school,' he announced after his first day at Salisbury Street.

'Well you've gotta goo whether you like it or not,' Annie retorted. Tom said no more but his face wore a mutinous look. The next morning, however, he submitted meekly enough as his mother helped him dress for school. When he asked her for a ha'penny to buy a few sweets from Sleath's, her face softened and she handed him the money. 'Goo on then,' she smiled as she pushed him gently towards the door. 'Be a good lad for the teacher and goo straight to school.'

Tom walked along the road between George and Nellie. They would accompany him as far as Station Street and would then turn left to the Stepping Bridge, while Tom continued right towards Salisbury Street.

It was half past nine that morning and Annie was just banging the hearth rug against the brewhouse wall, when Tom appeared with cheek bulging, round the entry. Annie dropped the rug in dismay and advanced upon her young son. 'Why aint you in school?' she demanded. Tom gazed back defiantly. 'I towd thee yesterday, I doe like it theer.'

Annie caught hold of his arm and frogmarched him down the entry. Her face was grim as she handed him over to his teacher. 'I should keep yer eye on 'im,' she advised, 'else he'll be off agen the minit yer back's turned.'

Annie sighed as she trudged back up Station Street. 'Nearly a mornin' wasted,' she muttered to herself. 'He'd better not try that one on agen.' She had a very soft spot for her youngest son but she had to admit that he was fast becoming a handful. And his language! 'Comes of hangin' around the men, listening to their talk,' she thought crossly. Tom played truant twice more that week and when he again asked his mother for a ha'penny on Friday morning she turned on him in fury.

'I'll gi' thee a bloody ha'penny all right. 'Ere,' she turned to George, 'Run to Harvey's quick an' get me a ha'penny cane.' The cane was thin and very supple and Annie applied it to the back of Tom's legs all the way along Bull Street, Gladstone Street and the length of Station Street. When they eventually reached the corner of Salisbury Street, Tom went skipping into the school entrance with an alacrity which would have warmed the heart of any teacher.

The cane was put away in the cupboard as a silent deterrent, but it seemed that Tom had learned his lesson and played truant no more.

Nellie still saw a good deal of Edie Clamp but since moving to Tilley Street she had made a number of new friends. Violet Jakes and Annie Harper, who lived in nearby Whitton Street, were two who were to remain her constant companions for many years. She also found the time to amuse Gladys Whitehouse, the mentally disabled and only child of their next-door neighbours. Gladys was able to join in a few of their games and Nellie always treated the girl with gentle consideration and had a protective feeling towards her. Hilda Lester was a girl with whom Nellie and the others always tried to curry favour. Her father was publican of the Engine Inn on Bull Piece. Hilda possessed a very fine swing and would sometimes allow a few privileged among her friends to enter the pub's front entrance, walk over the sawdust-strewn floor to the little paved yard at the rear, to enjoy the blissful delights of the much-coveted swing.

# 9

# Pastimes & Tradesmen

Many and varied were the games played by the girls and boys of Nellie's childhood years. They played Tin Can Alerky and a game called Tip Cat, for which they required a piece of wood, perhaps cut from a broomstick. This would be sharpened at both ends and placed on the ground. The player would then strike one end sharply to see how far the stick could be made to fly. Most of the boys possessed an iron hoop which had a handle. This would be pushed along at a spanking pace, while the girls would usually make do with a wooden hoop, which could be purchased from Harvey's shop for 4*d*.

The boys would play marbles on the dusty brick pavements while the girls plied their skipping ropes, chanting all the old traditional rhymes.

A pastime common to both, during March in particular, was the flying of kites on the windy Black Nob.

A game that often caused trouble was hop scotch, as some of the women would object to the chalk lines drawn on the pavement outside their front doors. However, a few of the younger mothers, Annie included, were sometimes to be seen lifting their skirts above their ankles and hopping with great agility, to the delight of their grinning offspring. Nellie and her friends also enjoyed playing with their whips and tops. A whip could be bought for a penny, while the top, with its many coloured rings, cost only a halfpenny.

Nellie loved the long summer evenings, when neighbours would gather to gossip for hours on their front doorsteps and their children played out late in the streets unhindered. Sometimes they would be sent off to the pub with large china jugs to fetch frothing beer, which would be enjoyed with the supper, eaten on front doorsteps. On Whit Monday the men would take a rope end and turn it slowly while the women showed off their skipping ability amid noisy encouragement from their children and their more sedentary neighbours who preferred to watch.

The street in which Nellie lived had visits from a variety of tradespeople, each adding a flash of colour and interest to her life. There was a couple from Gornal named Mr and Mrs Watton, and Nellie would always remember the old lady, who wore a poke bonnet, and her husband, who sported a red spotted muffler. They would sit side by side on their horse-drawn cart, shouting loudly, 'Do yer want any sond or salt?' and the women would come out of their houses to buy sandstones and bathbrick and the rough salt hewn from blocks.

The knife sharpener would appear, pushing his cycle with its grinding wheel and sometimes the hurdy-gurdy man would be seen, filling the street with gay music, accompanied by a tiny sad-eyed monkey. On one occasion great excitement was caused when a man and his dancing bear arrived. The children were thrilled by the sight of the huge brown animal, shambling along on its hind legs, safely tethered with a heavy collar and chain.

A familiar figure was the lamplighter, who trudged the streets night and morning bearing a long pole. Then there was the little old man who was paid 6d to tap with a long stick on the windows of those folk who needed to be knocked up of a morning. An annual event to look forward to by everyone was Darlaston Wakes. This was always held on the nearest Saturday to 25 July on a stretch of land near to the old tram sheds, next to Pitchers the Wheelwrights. The fair would continue for a week to ten days and was considered an occasion of such importance that the women would make preparations for weeks in advance. Their rooms would be re-papered, curtains freshly washed and flower pots red ochred with Cardinal, costing 6d a tin, to show off the geraniums which decked the window sills.

New clothes were bought by those who could afford them and many of the women would wear a new straw hat. Some of them however, preferred a man's cap secured with a hat pin.

A special traditional meal would be prepared; duck served with new potatoes and garden peas. Annie and Jim usually took their family to the fair on the Monday afternoon and Annie would pack a large basket for a picnic tea. They would spend the whole of the afternoon and evening at the fair, returning at dusk, very tired but blissfully happy.

# 10

# War

World affairs rarely intruded into Annie's life, but she could not help but be aware that the country was moving inevitably towards conflict with Germany. When war was finally declared on 4 August 1914, she gradually became accustomed to the departure of one after another of her neighbours, answering the call to give service to King and Country. The idea of Jim following their example never once entered her head until he came home one fine October day and announced somewhat sheepishly that he had joined the army. Annie glanced up from her sewing. 'What army?' she asked. 'The Salvation Army?'

'No, me wench,' Jim replied. 'I've just accepted the King's shillin''.

'You've done what?' she cried, dropping her sewing. 'Oh yer bloody fool, Jim, whatever med yer do that?' Annie's eyes filled with tears. 'Oh Jim,' she cried again, 'Whatever med yer do it?'

Jim sat down and pulled her onto his lap. 'Come on owd gel, doe yer cry, I'd probably get called up before long, an' anyway, yer know there aint much work around so I might as well goo now.'

'But 'ow shall we manage?' she sobbed, her anger rising sharply as she pictured herself coping alone with the children, trying to manage without Jim's support. 'But yer didn't 'ave ter do it,' she shouted struggling to her feet. 'I expect as somebody put it inter yer 'ead, one o' yer drinkin' pals.'

As this was very nearly the truth, Jim got up, reaching for his cap. 'I'm gooin' ter see Sam,' he muttered making for the door. If he stayed any longer, Annie would get properly worked up, so he'd best make himself scarce until she'd had time to cool off.

Later on he was telling Sam why he'd actually joined up. He had been sitting in The Vine with some of his pals discussing the latest war news when Teecy put down his pint and asked nobody in particular 'Wot's the war about, that's wot I'd like to know?'

Nobody answered immediately, each waiting for the next man to explain. Finally an old man sitting by himself in the corner removed his pipe from between his teeth and spoke up. 'We'm fightin' cause Germany went fer Belgium. It's got nothin' at all ter do wi' we, it's them toffynosed gits we sends ter parlyment wot's let we in fer it an' it meks me proper sick.' He stuck his pipe back into his mouth and sucked on it fiercely.

A murmur went round the room which indicated that many of those present were in agreement with this opinion.

'Well, I doe know,' said Jim thoughtfully. 'It seems ter me like this, supposin' I was ter see a couple o' blokes punchin' 'ell out o' your missis an' I took no notice an' sed it weren't nuthin ter do wi' me, well you'd none on yer think much o' me would yer?' Jim looked enquiringly into the faces of his pals but getting no response, continued earnestly. 'Doe yer see that's just what's 'appenin' ter Belgium an' that's why we've joined in.'

'But why should we fight at all?' protested Herbert. 'Germany 'ad no quarrel wi' we.'

'Ar, but I bet we'd 'ave bin next in line once the Germans 'ad finished,' argued Jim. 'An' besides, a country doe always 'ave ter fight fer itself. Sometimes it 'as ter defend people too weak ter defend themselves.'

After further animated discussion which required plenty of refreshment for throats parched with much talking, the general opinion veered towards Jim's point of view. Indeed it was generally agreed that those miserable sods who failed to volunteer and fight the Huns deserved to be despised by their families and friends.

Swollen with beer and patriotic fervour, the group made its way to the nearest recruiting centre, where they each underwent a medical examination. Out of the original twelve, who had taken up the challenge, only Jim and two others were passed as fit.

One week later Annie and the children accompanied Jim to the Drill Hall in Church Street to join the other families who were there to wave goodbye to the departing soldiers. Jim looked grand in khaki, thought Annie, and how tall and straight he stood, with his hair closely cut and moustache neatly trimmed. The children clung to their father's legs, as they waited for the time of departure. Nellie had cried herself to sleep when she learned that he was going away. George had said very little but he felt sick inside at the thought of his father's leaving. However, when Jim put his hand on the boy's shoulder and told him that he must look after his mother and the others, he looked proudly into his father's eyes and promised to do his best.

*Jim Askey, fourth left on the middle row.*

'I should get a leave soon Annie,' Jim assured her, 'once trainin's over.'

'Yer mean before they send yer ter France,' said Annie in a choked voice.

'Well, it woe be fer long,' said Jim cheerfully.

'Long enough ter get yerself killed,' replied Annie bitterly. She had not really forgiven Jim for enlisting although she'd tried hard not to reproach him again after her initial outburst.

Nellie clutched her father's hand tightly until the very last minute, when he'd picked her up in his arms and held her tightly before kissing her goodbye. Then he turned to his wife, 'Look after yerself me wench, I'll write as soon as I'm settled.' He kissed her once more and then knelt down to kiss Tom and Evelyn. Tom started to bawl loudly and after trying unsuccessfully to quiet him, Jim was thankful when the order came to fall in and he ran off quickly to join his comrades of the 6th South Staffs.

In the weeks that followed, Jim, who was stationed at Harrogate in Yorkshire, had only one leave before embarking for France the following February. During this leave another baby was conceived. She was born in June and Annie had her christened Mary Irene but the child was so lovely with pale blond hair and huge blue eyes that everyone called her Beauty.

Jim never saw his little girl for when she was one year and ten months old she caught meningitis and very soon afterwards followed her sister, Lizzie, into James Bridge Cemetery. Annie was given a note to be taken to the Police Station in order that a message might be dispatched requesting compassionate leave for Jim. Annie handed the note to Sergeant Hull, who glanced at it and enquired 'How old was the child?'

'A year and ten months,' faltered Annie, tears springing into her eyes.

'Oh, a mere baby,' observed the sergeant, dismissing the grief-stricken mother without a trace of sympathy.

Beauty had been dead for six months before Jim received the news. One of the first things he did when he eventually returned home was to march up to the Police Station to seek out Sergeant Hull. 'Buller' Askey, tall and tough-looking in his uniform, was a formidable sight and a look of fear sprang into the sergeant's eyes, when Jim caught hold of him none too gently and told him exactly what he thought of Hull's callous treatment of a serving man's wife, a man who was fighting for the likes of police sergeants, who were able to remain in safety at home.

# 11

# On the Move Again

After the death of her beautiful little daughter, Annie seemed to change. Although she had experienced grief before with the loss of Lizzie and Grandad Tom, somehow she had managed to recover and carry on with life much as before. Now, with Jim away and the burden of struggling to feed the family, the death of Beauty had come as a devastating blow. Her face took on a defeated, weary look and her voice grew sharper. George and Nellie noticed the change more than the younger two. For them at least, Annie still managed to find some affection but it seemed, to Nellie most of all, that her mother no longer cared for her and was attempting in some way to rid herself of her misery by inflicting it upon George and herself. George, a quiet thoughtful boy, resentful of his mother's attitude and her unfairness to Nellie, would try to comfort her awkwardly, when she would run off by herself to cry, after Annie had set about her in a fury.

'Praps her woe be soo bad when feyther gets 'ome,' he'd say, trying to convince himself at the same time. But as the days passed, Annie's attitude to them hardened, her mouth tightened into a grim line and the brother and sister grew to fear her violent tempers.

To be fair, Annie had more than a little to contend with. It was not easy trying to feed and clothe four children with such limited means. She had to look at every penny before it was spent and find ways of filling her family's bellies for next to nothing. She would send George to Clapps on the Walsall road for six penn'orth of specked fruit and would remove the bad from a few apples to make a pie with the remainder. Nellie would take a basket to Moreton's cake shop in King Street and stand patiently in a long queue for a bag of stale cakes. From Dingley's on the corner of Cobden Street they would buy 3d of bacon bits and 3d of grey peas, which provided a substantial meal. On Thursday afternoons one of the children would fetch the large china jug from the washstand in Annie's bedroom and carry it to Kingston's butcher's shop. Mrs Kingston would make a

*Clapps' shop on the Walsall road.*

*Dingley's on the corner of Cobden Street.*

tasty soup in a wash boiler and dole it out in proportionate measures, depending on the size of each family. On Saturday afternoons, Nellie would be off to 'Daddy' West, the Vicar of All Saints' Church to receive a half-crown 'for soldiers' wives'. Breakfast on Saturday mornings consisted of stale bread and crusts put into a

*'Daddy' West's Vicarage.*

basin and soaked in tea with a little sugar and milk added, since Annie could not afford to use milk only.

In addition to keeping her own home clean, Annie now cleaned and washed for a family called Hickman.

When there was to be a particularly large wash Annie kept Nellie from school to help her. The child stood on a box so that she could reach the tub to pound the clothes with the 'maid'. She then had to help her mother to feed the wet heavy clothes through the mangle, afterwards folding them neatly into the clothes basket. Nellie dreaded these wash days when it seemed that her thin little arms would never stop aching and her hands were alternately frozen and scalded.

One day Annie heard through a neighbour of an empty house in Whitton Street. As it had three bedrooms and was much larger than theirs, she decided it was time for a move. The landlord was named Mr Austin and he collected the rents on Monday mornings. The following Monday she took Evelyn and Tom and waited on the corner of the street to catch him. Mr Austin agreed to let her have the key and it was decided that they would move in immediately.

It was December and the weather was bitterly cold. It snowed heavily the night before they left and the following morning, the snow was still falling. George was despatched to Bob Smith's to procure a handcart, on which most of the larger furniture was piled.

*Whitton Street.*

*No. 23 Whitton Street.*

George and Nellie helped their mother to push it, while Tom and Evelyn struggled behind with more household items packed into a battered old pram. Fortunately Whitton Street was just around the next corner from their old home but it required all their combined strength to push the cart through the heavy snow. When they arrived at no. 23 they found it impossible to get up the entry and round to the back door as the snow was up to the window sills. Eventually, completely exhausted, although quite warm with their efforts, Annie and the children succeeded in piling all their belongings into the front room. The youngsters wandered about the empty rooms, almost speechless with awe at their size, which seemed to them enormous compared to the cramped quarters of Tilley Street. The front room had the usual black firegrate and floorboards which would require a great deal of scrubbing to bring them up to Annie's standard of cleanliness.

Beyond this room was the kitchen, a good sized square room with wall cupboards, a large black-leaded fireplace and red quarry tiles. A narrow passage led out to the small scullery which had a firegrate with a boiler and a brown stone sink underneath the window. There would be just enough room for the mangle and tub and Annie's black iron cooking stove. The stairs went up from the middle passage. Off the long landing with its queer little step in the middle, was a front bedroom for Jim and Annie. The girls would share the middle room and George and Tom would occupy the smaller back bedroom overlooking the party yards and brewhouses, which huddled together with the same regular drabness.

'I doe know how I'm gonna fill all these rooms wi' our few sticks,' sighed Annie looking around, 'but I expect it'll look awright when we gets a bit straight. Any road it's too late to do much more today, let's lay these mattresses on the floor an' we'll manage down 'ere tonight.'

'I'm 'ungry' complained Tom, 'can we 'ave summat to eat now?'

'I doe know what thee cost 'ave,' said Annie. 'I 'ad ter pay a shillin' for the handcart.' After further thought she remembered the packet of Bird's Custard powder. She made a large jugful, so thick you could have cut it with a knife, but it helped to fill their bellies and when they'd all had a saucerful each they settled down to sleep, tired out with the day's doings.

Eventually, by dint of much hard work and elbow grease, the house was put to rights. Nellie and George had no time for play in the few days that followed their arrival in Whitton Street. Annie kept them hard at it. The floorboards in the front room had to be scrubbed repeatedly with hot water and soft brown soap before Annie was satisfied. The grates were black-leaded and brushed until they acquired a high sheen, and all the windows were cleaned inside and out. Nellie's knees became red and painful as she moved from step to step of the stairs, scrubbing as she went. George and the younger children were put to work clearing a path from the back door to the outside lavatory and the entry.

The house was very cold in spite of the fire which was kept going all day and banked up at night. The bedrooms in particular were freezing and Nellie and Evelyn would huddle together in an effort to find warmth. Annie felt Jim's absence more keenly than ever but she was so tired at night that she fell asleep almost immediately.

The family gradually became accustomed to the house and soon appreciated the extra space, although Nellie sometimes thought longingly of the little house in Tilley Street, which held for her so many happy memories of her father. However, life was not altogether unhappy and, while the snow lasted, the children had fun pelting each other with snowballs. One particular morning they opened all the doors and flung snowballs right through the house. As Annie, standing in the scullery, happened to be in one of her rare good moods, she just laughed at them indulgently and threw them back with a return of her old high spirits.

# 12

# Christmas

As Christmas approached, their hearts grew lighter. Jim had written that he hoped to be home and the family could hardly wait to see him. Annie had always made much of Christmas and took a great deal of trouble to make her money stretch as far as possible to giver her family pleasure. Nobody had a Christmas tree, but instead would use the thin wooden strips which encircled tubs of butter, bought from the Maypole in King Street. These were fastened together to form a crown and would then be covered with six penn'orth of coloured tissue paper. When that was done, it was hung about with a variety of goodies, sugar mice, pigs, clocks and churches, fruit and small toys. Annie had hers suspended from a hook screwed into the ceiling, where it swung around each time the door opened. Two weeks before Christmas, Bob Smith would decorate his 'Favourite House' shop windows. This was a sight to behold and parents would take their excited children to the shop in Church Street to stand and gape with popping eyes at all its splendours. The window facing onto Bilston Street would be dressed with many coloured lights but the larger window contained such a vast display of toys that it looked like Aladdin's Cave. Mothers of naughty children could immediately restore good behaviour with the threat that, 'if yer doe behave yerself yer woe goo an' see Bob Smith's winder.'

Bob Smith himself would don his Father Christmas costume and stand in the doorway of the shop. At his side were placed two bran sacks concealing little toys for a penny dip. He would ask each child 'is yer dad a sojer?' If the answer was 'yes', he would then reach into a particular sack for the dip. The kids soon cottoned on, however, and Bob's question was always answered in the affirmative. If a child looked fairly prosperous however, he would receive his dip from the other sack. Children never expected a lot anyway. The most that they could hope for in their stockings would be a new penny, an orange, an apple, a new pair of stockings from Appleyard's costing 6½d or perhaps a new pinner. There would be a few toys too, of course, possibly a post office set, tiny cups and saucers or perhaps a sweet shop, all of which could be bought very cheaply at the penny bazaar.

Christmas Eve, and Annie sat dejectedly in her kitchen, surrounded by the children. She had now given up hope that Jim would be home for Christmas, but she had still made an effort to make some preparations, by decorating the spotless house and hiding away a few things for the children's stockings. There would be no proper Christmas dinner, of course, with a roast fowl. They would have to make do with a rabbit. Annie got up to light the oil lamp which hung from the ceiling, 'Well, it woe be much of a Christmas this year,' she remarked. 'An' doe expect a lot in yer stockin's either. If yer dad could've bin 'ere, things woulda bin different.'

George had been sitting with head bent staring at the floor. He'd been studying the way in which the lamp was casting shadows onto the tiles. After some time he looked up and said, 'Look, mother, can yer see? It looks just like a picture of me dad.'

Annie stared at the floor, following George's pointing finger. 'Goo an' fetch a pinch o' whitenin' out o' the back quick,' she told him.

George rubbed the chalky substance into the floor, carefully following the outlines. When he had finished Annie looked amazed, he was right, it looked just like Jim, even his moustache. She burst into tears. 'It's an omen,' she cried. 'I'm sure as he's bin killed!' The children immediately began to cry too, becoming so distraught that Annie pulled herself together. 'Nellie!' she said, 'Goo an' fetch Mrs Hancox an' Mrs Duckhouse.' These were her nearest neighbours with whom she'd become quite friendly.

The two women 'ooh'd and arr'd' and agreed that it did indeed look like Jim Askey, having known him for a number of years. Although they secretly agreed with Annie that it could indeed be an omen of death, they tried their best to cheer everybody up and stayed for a cup of tea and a gossip.

Later, the house was dark and silent. The fire banked up to be poked into life the next morning cast a flickering red glow into the room, revealing the chalk outline Annie had insisted should be left on the floor. Four bulky stockings dangled from the mantelpiece. The heavy slow tick-tock of the clock and the occasional chink as a bit of coal fell, were the only sounds in the room. The hands of the clock pointed to 1.00 a.m. as the first thunderous knocks shook the front door and awakened the house.

'Mother, mother!' called George, 'there's somebody knockin' the door!'

'Well, let 'em bloody knock,' shouted Annie. 'I ain't gerrin' up in the middle o' the night.'

'I'll goo down an' see who it is,' said George and he ran shivering down the stairs and struggled to open the front door. He took one unbelieving look at the tall figure wearing a tin helmet, who stood in the darkness, then he sprang at his father, yelling, 'It's me dad, it's me dad!'

The rest of the family came tumbling downstairs and the children danced around on cold bare feet, laughing and crying as their mother and father embraced. The lamp was re-lit, the fire poked into life and the kettle put on. Evelyn pointed to the chalk and said, 'Me mother said it meant as you'd bin killed.' Jim laughed saying it would take more than a few Huns to kill him.

The children were later ushered back to bed reluctantly, but overjoyed that their dad was home for Christmas. Annie and Jim sat contentedly by the fireside, exchanging news, until Jim took her hand and murmured, 'Annie, I've got summat to tell yer. It's about Ben.' Ben was Annie's youngest brother and they had always been close.

'Why, wot's the matter wi' 'im?' asked Annie fearfully.

'I'm afraid as he's dead,' Jim replied gently.

'Oh, he can't be, Kath would've said,' cried Annie.

'He is, me wench. He was wi' me in the trenches when we went over the top. He needn't have gone, yer know, bein' an officer's bat man, but 'e turned to me an' said, "If thee bist gooin', Jim, soo am I." We went over together an' 'e was killed almost immediately. When we got back I found 'im an' I 'elped to bury 'im.' Jim put his hand into his pocket and withdrew a small metal object, handing it to Annie. 'That's 'is cap badge, the Sherwood Foresters. I 'ad to 'and all 'is other belongin's in but I kep' the badge.'

'Oh, Jim, where will it all end?' she sobbed. 'Mr Whitehouse is dead, as well. Dost remember how 'e used ter sing ter Mrs Whitehouse, "When the Fields are white with Daisies and the Roses bloom again?" Now her's left wi' just that poor child.'

'I'm sorry I 'ad ter tell yer Annie, but I wanted to tell yer meself before yer see Kath.'

'I know,' Annie whispered, 'but we woe tell the kids. Let 'em enjoy Christmas now you'm home.'

'Come on old gel,' said Jim getting wearily to his feet. 'We'd best get off ter bed or we'll both be wore out termorrow.'

Jim was up early on Christmas morning. He left the house and returned later with a large fowl, which he had managed to buy somewhere. Quite a few shops remained open that morning so Jim was able to buy presents for Annie and the children. The enormous fowl was taken to the bake house in Bull Street and the family's Christmas dinner was the best they had ever had.

All too soon it was over. Jim returned to the Front, this time to Italy. The parting was hard and Nellie and George in particular dreaded their father leaving them. Since coming home he had been a softening influence on their mother and there had been some return of the old family atmosphere. When Jim left the house however, it seemed that all the warmth had gone with him. Annie at first appeared to be sunk within herself, displaying no interest in life or the energy to cope with it, but the children had to eat and the habit of work was too strong in her for Annie to remain apathetic for long.

She started work at Boyes and Bodin's, a timber works in Station Street, making railway sleepers. Annie's job was to creosote the sleepers and after a while the children got used to the unfamiliar pungent smell she brought home with her. She also brought home bits of the sleepers which were burnt to help out the quarter of coal and two penn'orth of slack which George and Nellie would fetch from Cooper's coal yard at the bottom of Tilley Street, pushing it home in a small trolley with iron wheels.

The children were at school during most of Annie's working hours. She would pop back home at dinner time to feed them, but would not return until after 5.30 at night. Woe betide Nellie and George if they did not run straight home from school in order to make sure that the fire was burning well, the house clean and the table set ready for tea. They both knew only too well what a hammering they would receive if they were not in the house, all tasks completed before their mother returned. It often seemed hard to them that in winter when school was dismissed, their mates would stay out, sliding and sledging, while they must run straight home to a cold dark house.

Life was particularly hard for Nellie, for in addition to the work she had to do at home, Annie had arranged for her to take dinner each day to Mr Constable, who worked at the Patent Shaft in Wednesbury. It meant that when Nellie came out of school at twelve o'clock she would have to run all the way to the Constable's house opposite Bass's on the Walsall road. Mrs Constable would be waiting for her with dinner all ready in a wicker basket, with a rice pudding in a cloth balanced on top and secured with a clothes peg. For Nellie's dinner she provided a slice of bread spread thickly with mashed potatoes and gravy with another slice on top. She would have to eat this as she ran along. Mrs Constable gave Nellie a penny for the tram fare from the Bull Stake, but on fine days she would keep the money and run instead along the back of the Old Park to Wednesbury. She would buy two halfpenny oranges from a little shop in the Portway Road after delivering Mr Constable's dinner, then she would run on again, not stopping until she arrived breathlessly back at school. Nellie received one shilling in payment for this task and was expected to hand every penny of it to her mother each Friday.

It was such a long way to run each day from the Central School that Nellie decided she would leave and try All Saints' which was just across the road from her house. It was an easy matter to arrange and it seemed to Nellie at first to have been a good move. However, she very soon discovered that she hated the school; most of the girls came from well-off families and wore nice clothes, in sharp contrast to Nellie's somewhat ill-assorted garments.

She had been in attendance for nearly three months on the morning she entered the classroom wearing, for her, quite a smart dress given to Annie by the lady whose washing she did. One of the girls pointed to her and exclaimed in a very carrying voice. 'Oh, look at Nellie Askey, her's wearing one of Frances Hickman's frocks!' Under the gaze of the other 'young ladies' Nellie turned scarlet. She stood in acute embarrassment before rushing out of the door and out of the school.

'I'm not gooin' back theer,' she told her mother. 'They all used ter sneer at me cloes before but at least they was me own. If I've got to wear Frances Hickman's frocks, I'll wear 'em at a different school.'

So back she went to the Central School prepared to run the extra distance to avoid the taunts of her former school mates.

Nellie had delivered Mr Constable's dinners for twelve months and then another job was found for her.

Every Friday afternoon as soon as she got home from school, she would run round to the Yates' house next door, leaving George to carry on with the usual jobs at home. She would then spend two and a half hours of really hard cleaning. First she would black-lead the grate and rub up the fire irons. The next job would be on her knees scrubbing the quarry tiles of the large kitchen. Next was the veranda, which had to be swept out and wiped down. Finally, she would tackle the brewhouse, out in the cold. For her week's labours Nellie was paid one shilling and sixpence and her mother took every penny. Sometimes as she scrubbed the floor, the sounds of children's laughter came to her from the street or the backyards and tears would roll down her cheeks and fall into the bucket. She felt so unloved that at times her misery was just too much to bear.

Her hands that should have been the soft unlined hands of childhood, were already red and roughened like an old woman's. It seemed that no matter how hard she worked and how much she tried to please her mother, her efforts failed. Annie would extend her hand for the money, with no word of praise and rewarding smile. How Nellie longed for her father, although on occasions he was strict and did not hesitate to hit out if one of them went too far, he was always fair-minded. The children never doubted that he loved them, but Nellie often wondered if her mother loved her at all.

# 13

# 'Come Quick, Me Mother's got the Bellyache'

Annie was pregnant again. The discovery brought quick dismay and a stab of fierce resentment but later on she was able to accept it philosophically enough. She prayed that the war would be ended soon, bringing Jim safely home. His letters were somewhat irregular and he never mentioned that he had been gassed in Italy. They were filled instead with details of the day-to-day combat with lice which infected every seam of clothing; when he came home on leave, Annie had to run a hot iron along the seams to kill them. He also wrote of the good comradeship to be found amid the horror and the mud of the trenches.

His letters always ended with his love to his children and his praise of Annie for caring for them so well. Jim never discovered, for Nellie and George did not tell him, of their mother's lack of feeling and her behaviour that at times amounted to cruelty.

One evening in early April, the sun had at last appeared after a day of continuous showers, bringing out of the houses the children for an hour or two's games before bed. No play for Nellie, she rubbed her sore knees with a wet hand. Her mother had been in a vicious mood all day and Nellie's reddened ear still smarted from the blows it had received. She was told to scrub down the stairs and 'mek a good job on it or else!'

She had just reached the bend, nearly at the top of the stairs when Annie, who had been having a 'lay' down appeared at the top, doubled over, clutching her swollen belly. Nellie looked up startled, the dripping scrubbing brush in her hand.

'Wot's the matter mother?' she cried in alarm, frightened by the screwed up look of pain on Annie's face. 'Goo an' fetch our Sally,' gasped Annie. 'Tell 'er to come straight away an' send somebody for Nurse Shaw.'

As Nellie flew downstairs and out into the entry she had no idea what was happening to her mother. The facts of life were as unknown to her as they were to most children of her age. Indeed, some newly married women were nearly as ignorant.

When at last she came panting to the door of her young married cousin, who lived nearby, she implored her to 'come quick, me mother's got the belly ache!'

Sally, a sensible girl of nineteen, asked no questions but quickly dispatched one of her neighbours to alert the nurse before following swiftly at Nellie's heels.

As they reached the back door, Sally, hearing Annie's anguished cries above, restrained Nellie at the foot of the stairs and told her to make a cup of tea. Then, as she reached the bedroom door, she was just in time to see the baby's head emerging from Annie's pain-racked body. Sally coped with the situation beautifully, although totally inexperienced in the process of birth. She behaved with the competence of a woman twice her age, at what was to be the first of many births she would attend in the course of her long, long life.

Downstairs in the little scullery, Nellie was just placing the cups on the table when the thin reedy cry of the newborn infant reached her astonished ears. A few minutes later Sally, somewhat shaken but triumphant by her experience, announced to Nellie that she had a new little sister. Nellie burst into tears. She ran into the kitchen and cried her heart out.

'Wot's up wi' thee then?' asked Sally. Nellie raised her tear-streaked face.

'Poor mother,' she sobbed, 'fancy 'avin' a babby wi' me Dad soo far away.'

Annie's last child was a bonny, placid baby, who gave her mother little trouble. She was christened Marie and her brothers and sisters adored her. During the long summer holidays, Nellie would put her in Tom's old pushchair and push her for hours along the leafy lanes and flower starred hedges; minding Marie was a job she never tired of. Sometimes she and Violet Jakes or Annie Harper would set off on a fine morning with Marie in the pushchair and a bag containing some jam sandwiches and a bottle of cold tea. They would walk all the way

*Jim, Marie, Evelyn and Annie.*

to Wolverhampton and Marie would sit contentedly, sucking at her bottle of milk and gurgling at passers-by until they finally reached the town. If they were lucky they would be given a copper or two to spend on sweets and after a short walk around the small close-packed shops, it would be time to start the long walk home. They would arrive at tea-time, footsore and weary but satisfied with the day's outing.

There were lots of children in Whitton Street. There was a little boy called 'Winkie' Small, who always wore a red fez; his proper name was Wilfred. There were two sisters named Sally and Phoebe Shakespeare. It was Sally who taught Nellie, at the age of ten, to crochet with a nail until Nellie became proficient at making curtain loops and mantle fringes from pretty coloured silks. There were Hector, Hope, Frank and Ted Etchells, Billy and Phoebe Banks, Anna and Ted Davies, Floss and Sam Wilkes and Winnie Gibbons. These were the children whom Nellie remembered, and many years later, if she happened to meet one of these faces from the past, they would immediately say, 'Dost remember when we went scrap pickin?'

Hector and Frank Etchells and Teddy Davis, together with Nellie, Violet Jakes and Annie Harper often went picking scrap 'between the werks' near to Cottrell's in Station Street. The shop floors were swept clean of the 'strippings' from the nuts and bolts and these would be

*Picking coal.*

loaded onto a horse-drawn cart and dumped on a waste patch. The children, armed with long pieces of wire with hooks on the end were allowed to squat on the ground and pick over the scrap. The strippings were then collected and put into ''erden' (Hessian) bags. When they had collected sufficient, the children would take it along to 'Ole Shakespeare', who lived two doors away from Nellie. The children soon learned how to con the old man into paying twice over for the scrap. The girls would swipe the bags he had already paid for, while the boys kept him talking. He always argued over payment; then they would offer the same bags for sale the next time. All the money received however would be handed over to their mothers.

When the coal strike was on, everybody went coal picking. They would walk to Wednesbury carrying or pushing whatever receptacle they could find. It may have been an old pram or a box on wheels, but gangs of children would descend on the Old Park Road and spend the entire day there. Nellie loved those times. She would set off with the others taking the usual bottle of tea and bread and jam for dinner. The men, having dug a large hole to get at the coal, would shout to the waiting children 'Yo can pick in my dirt!' and the little 'uns would rush to squat on the ground, clucking like so many hens as they scrabbled in the dirt for bits of coal, getting grubbier and grubbier as the day wore on. Looking back, Nellie saw those days as among the happiest of her life.

# 14

# 'Bone Shakers'

Jim was demobbed in February 1919, after fighting valiantly, and comparatively unscathed, in many of the major battles of the war in France and Italy. His tin helmet was painted all around with the names of some of them; the Somme, Ypres, Rheims and Hill 60. The family was united once more and, at once, Jim's homecoming had a considerable effect on their lives. There was work in plenty and he started at once on a local building site. The financial burden was eased and Annie no longer had to hide behind the door when Mr Austin came to collect his rent. She was also able to buy one or two items of furniture she had long wanted for her home. The house, which had seemed at first so large and bare had gradually acquired a cosy comfort.

Annie bought some pretty lino for the front room to cover the bare boards, from Bishop Marsden's in King Street. From James Bass on Bull Piece she had purchased two pegged rugs costing 12*s* 6*d* for the two downstairs rooms, together with a rather large ornate chest of drawers. The shiny black leather sofa was placed underneath the window and a red chenille cloth covered the square table in the centre of the room. Annie's sewing machine stood on one side of the firegrate and a comfortable wooden armchair occupied the other. Pretty lace curtains covered the windows, caught back with crocheted loops done in pale pink silk by Nellie. The mantelshelf, with its matching red chenille cloth, held a few bright ornaments. Nellie no longer had to attend school clad in one of George's jumpers underneath her pinner or shod in a pair of his over-large boots.

One economy still practised, however, was to conceal holes in black stockings with an application of boot polish.

Although Nellie was much happier now that her father was home, Annie's attitude towards the child remained unchanged. Nothing that Nellie did was right in her mother's eyes. It seemed as if Annie was driven on by something inside her that took a peculiar pleasure in nagging and taunting the poor girl.

When, on occasion, Jim remonstrated with her about her unreasonable attitude, it only served to increase her fury. Jim, blind as ever to his wife's faults, would shrug his shoulders and assume that she knew best. He did try to compensate for Annie's behaviour towards her by trying to give Nellie extra attention. He would gently touch her hair and give her a few coppers to spend on sweets. If he happened to be at home when Nellie got in from school, he would skewer a bit of his bacon on the end of the poker and cook it over the fire for her. He would talk to her while it cooked and gradually the tight pinched look, which Nellie's face now habitually wore, relaxed and softened as she responded to his cheerful banter.

But if ever Annie happened to intrude on them unexpectedly, it served to put her into a bad humour and Jim gradually became aware that Annie was intensely jealous of any display of tenderness towards this particular daughter.

Home life became at times intolerable, with Annie deliberately trying to cause friction between Nellie and her father. She would untruthfully accuse the girl of some misdemeanour and in spite of Nellie's tearful protests, Jim was forced to take Annie's side.

Although school did not particularly appeal to her and she never shone academically, it did afford her some measure of relief from the tension at home. The only reward she ever received for school work was a banana, presented to her upon completing the best painting of the fruit.

A lesson she did enjoy was cookery. Every Friday all the local schools sent some of their pupils to the Central School for a cookery lesson. The mistress was a stout German woman named Miss Roscoe. The classroom had a long wooden table, which stood in the centre and was scrubbed scrupulously clean by four girls, working two on either side.

The cooking was done on an enormous range, which was black-leaded to shining perfection by each of the girls in turn.

One afternoon, a girl named Sally Harvey was instructed by Miss Roscoe to leave what she was doing and start to black-lead the range. After a few minutes hard work, Sally threw down the brush, shouting, 'That's it, I'm bloody fed up o' black-leadin' this thing an' I ay gonna do it no more!'

The scandalised teacher caned Sally good and hard, to the horrified enjoyment of the rest of the class. When it was over Sally ran out of the door. She returned later with her mother, a large sandy-haired woman, whose tongue was a good deal rougher than her appearance. After a most energetic slanging match before a delighted audience, punctuated by dire threats from Mrs Harvey as to what she would do if another finger was laid on 'her wench', the interview was terminated with the banning of Sally from all future cookery lessons.

On Sunday evenings when the weather was mild, a pleasurable occupation for Darlaston folks was listening to the band in Victoria Park.

Nellie would often go with Violet and Annie Harper and the concerts were usually well attended by families and courting couples. The girls liked to get as near to the bandstand as possible and Violet, who had a great fondness for lemons sprinkled with salt, would take a couple with her to enjoy with the music. The sight of Violet sucking noisily on the lemons put the bandsmen right off their stroke and they found it impossible to blow with their teeth all on edge. At the finish they would give up. 'Gerroff yer cheeky young buggers,' they would shout, waving their instruments and the girls would just fall about laughing at their predicament.

Another popular Sunday pastime for the girls was a visit to Owd 'Orlick's yard in Wood Street. Mr Horlick hired out bicycles at 3d per hour. They were a motley collection, comprising just a frame and two wheels, no brakes or other such refinements and they were real bone shakers.

Nellie, Annie Harper and Violet Jakes were returning from a pleasant Sunday afternoon ride to Bentley Common. They cycled down Bentley Lane and had just approached the canal bridge. A gang of lads sat on the side of the bridge and as soon as they sighted the trio, they began to catcall and jeer. Nellie and Violet swept past without comment but Annie turned her head to retaliate. Caught off balance, her concentration gone, she shot straight into the murky water of the 'cut'.

It was not very deep, and she soon managed to struggle to the side but she was covered from head to foot in smelly green slime. The lads were helpless, they fell about yelling with laughter while Nellie and Violet stood uncertainly on the canal edge wondering what to do. The bike had sunk beneath the scummy depths but when they had sufficiently recovered, the boys helped to haul it out and give Annie a hand to clamber up onto the side. She stank to high heaven and stood there dripping miserably. Nellie and Violet tried their best to be sympathetic, but she looked so funny with her hair plastered to her head that they finally collapsed into helpless giggles.

'It's awright fer you two buggers,' she swore, 'yo con loff, me owd woman'll bloody kill me when her sees me!'

'Never mind Annie,' chuckled Nellie. 'You can come 'ome wi' me an' get cleaned up a bit fust.'

They retrieved their bikes and mounted, Nellie and Violet giggling again at Annie's stiff-legged discomfiture.

When they arrived back at Owd 'Orlick's yard, they stopped at the gate and with a hard push, sent the bikes careering into the yard. They tore off down the road before Mr Horlick had a chance to discover the somewhat battered condition of one of his machines.

Nellie's mother was canting to Mrs Duckhouse when they emerged from the entry. The two women looked at Annie in surprise. 'Wot's thee bin doin' then?' grinned Mrs Duck'us, 'bin fer a swim 'ave yer?'

Nellie quickly explained her friend's predicament to her mother, who laughed and said, 'Well, you'd best cum in an' we'll see if we can get some o' that muck off yer.'

The girl was stripped of her wet clothes and sat shivering in front of the fire wrapped in a blanket from Nellie's bed. The clothes were washed in the sink and then put to steam over the bow.

'It's a good job you've got 'lastic in them bloomer legs,' chuckled Annie as she draped them, 'or they'd 'ave bin full o' fish!'

# 15

# First Job

Jim was now employed at Horton's Nut and Bolt factory, bricklaying, installing machinery and doing various alterations. When Nellie left school at fourteen years of age her father managed to secure a job for her in the warehouse.

Annie was pleased at the prospect of an extra wage. She was never satisfied with the money earned by Jim and George, who was learning the trade of bricklaying from his father. Nellie was dismayed to discover that all her workmates in the warehouse were much older than herself and that quite a few of her former school friends had found jobs in Horton's factory.

Although the work in the warehouse was considerably cleaner and comparatively easier, after a few weeks, she asked Jim if she could change jobs and work in the factory too.

Jim was surprised, but agreed saying, 'Doe blame me if thee doesn't like it, me wench. Thee'st find it a lot diffrunt tappin' nuts than packin' 'em.'

On the last Friday of her job in the warehouse, Nellie walked home with some of the girls she would be joining on the factory floor on the following Monday morning. The other girls were wearing shawls which had been quite the fashion to wear upon starting work. Nellie noticed that Fanny Winsper and herself were the only two wearing a coat. She mentioned this to Fanny and Fanny replied that her mother was buying a shawl for her tomorrow. 'I towd 'er that all the other wenches 'ad got shawls an' I day want ter be the odd one out.'

She looked at Nellie somewhat pityingly, 'Will yer mom let you 'ave one as well?' she asked.

Nellie had her doubts but she intended to ask right away, for it was unthinkable that all her mates should have shawls and she be the only one wearing a coat on Monday morning.

It was late Saturday evening before Nellie finally decided to mention the shawl to her mother, putting it off all day because of

Annie's mood. To begin with she had seemed in quite a good humour, even laughing a little over some bit of gossip imparted by a neighbour, but a little while later she said sharply, 'It's about time them crocks was washed up!' so Nellie had begun the washing-up and was stacking the dirty plates ready for immersion when they slid over and crashed into the stone sink.

Annie bounded into the scullery, her face contorted with anger. 'Wot's thee bangin' about at?' she shouted at Nellie. 'If thee doesn't want ter wash the bloody things up just leave 'em be! I suppose yer think as now you'm werkin' you'm entitled ter leave it all ter somebody else!'

This was grossly unfair and Annie knew it. Nellie never once complained about the amount of work she did at home, although she was well aware that she did far more than was expected of most girls of her age.

'It was an accident,' she protested. 'I doe mind doin' the washin' up, they slipped inter the sink before I could catch 'em.'

'Huh,' said Annie and stalked into the kitchen. Nellie felt despair well up inside her. She knew that now her mother was in one of her moods she would continue to add up her grievances and find fault with everything she did. The hope of getting her mother to agree to buy a shawl was remote indeed.

She completed her task, making sure that the scullery was in perfect order, knowing that her mother was sitting in sullen silence just waiting to have another go at her. The girl was tempted to slip through the back door and seek out Violet or Annie but the longing for a shawl made her desperate, for it was getting very late.

She swallowed her nervousness and went into the kitchen. As she supposed, her mother sat by the fire, her foot tapping, a sure indication of her annoyance.

Nellie sat down opposite her mother, clasping her hands in an old childish gesture.

'Honestly mother, I day'nt mean to bang the crocks,' she began.

'Humph,' snorted Annie, 'you'm always pullin' yer face when I ask yer to do anythin'. If you 'ad your way you'd be gaddin' off wi' them friends o' yourn all the time.'

The tapping foot increased its tempo and Nellie knew it was hopeless to argue or point out that when she was Evelyn's age she did a damned sight more than her sister ever did and that she and George worked much harder than anybody else.

They sat in silence for a while; glancing at her mother's stony face Nellie's courage almost failed her but the vision of a new shawl spurred her on to make another attempt.

'All the girls I'm gonna be workin' with on Monday 'ave all got shawls to wear,' she began.

'What dost expect me to do about it?' snapped Annie.

'Well, I thought I could get one,' said Nellie bravely. 'I doe want ter be the only one without.'

'Well yer thought wrong,' said Annie furiously. 'You'm gerrin' no shawl off me, yer must mek do wi' yer jacket an' be satisfied.' She got up, saying 'Tell yer dad when 'e comes in as I've popped ter see Ethel,' and she walked out, slamming the door behind her.

Nellie, although she had anticipated her mother's response, felt utterly dejected. 'It wasn't fair,' she thought bitterly. 'I never get anything new; I've never 'ad a new coat, me frocks am all second-hand an' even me undercloes am from the pawn shop.' She leaned her arms on the bow, put her head down on them and wept.

She just couldn't understand why her mother seemed to dislike her so much. It was true that Annie had always treated George too with the same unfairness but since he had started work her attitude towards him had undergone a distinct change. She never showed any affection for him but nevertheless she was much more reasonable with him now. Tom could always get away with murder. Not caring a toss, he would give his mother a mouthful of cheek and laugh at her. He was a happy-go-lucky lad and Annie tolerated a great deal from him. As for Evelyn and Marie nothing was too good for them and Annie found it easy to express affection for them both.

Reflecting on all this, Nellie didn't hear the back door open and was startled at the touch of a hand on her head.

'Hey up then, wot's thee blartin' for?' asked Jim.

Nellie raised her tear-streaked face. 'I asked mother if I could 'ave a shawl for werk like the rest on 'em, an' 'er says no,' she sniffed.

Jim sat down and began to unlace his boots. 'Is that all?' he asked. 'Goo an' mek me a cuppa tea, gel, an' blow thee nose.'

Something in his voice and the twinkle in his eye made Nellie's spirits surge upwards as she flew to obey him.

'Well now,' said Jim as, a little later on, he took a large gulp of the steaming tea. 'An' 'ow much do yer reckon as these shawls cost, eh?'

'4s 11d from Constables,' said Nellie hopefully.

Jim put down his cup and fumbled in his pocket. ''Ere you am,' he said, and withdrew two half crowns, he dropped them into Nellie's eager hand. 'You'd better run an' fetch one afore yer mother gets 'um.' He glanced at the clock on the mantelpiece. 'I day think it was that time,' he exclaimed, 'it's nearly eleven o'clock.'

'That's awright' Nellie assured him. 'They stop open until twelve.'

'Shall yer be awright on yer own?' he asked anxiously.

'Course I shall,' laughed Nellie, lightheared now as she skipped towards the door. 'I'll be back in a minute.'

The new shawl was grey plaid and Nellie wore it proudly on her first morning at the factory. Her feet were shod in heavy lace-up boots, into which Jim had hammered hob nails. Her working day began at 6.30 a.m. and ended at 5.30 p.m. Breakfast, consisting of bread and jam or dripping was eaten at half past eight as she sat at her machine and dinner was from half past twelve until half past one. Nellie was able to go home for this meal and on her first day at work had been given a whole egg for herself.

She enjoyed working with her old school friends; it made the day seem to go more quickly somehow. However, by the end of the first week her fingers were sore and bleeding but if she expected sympathy, she received none. 'They'll soon 'arden off,' the old 'uns told her. 'Dip 'em in the poe when thee gets 'um. That'll do the trick!'

Nellie had been at work for just a few weeks when there was a general strike. Together with her fellow workmates at Horton's she walked around the streets to all the local factories fetching the workers out by booing at the gates.

Her fingers had barely hardened off when Annie tackled her about money. Nellie's first week's pay was 9s 2d, and she received, as was the custom, a penny for every shilling she earned, but her mother was dissatisfied and told the girl to get another job. There was no shortage, so Nellie soon found work at Charles Richards Nut and Bolt factory in Heath Road and here her wages were increased to 12s 3d.

The foreman was George Anderson and he was generally disliked, but Nellie soon settled down with her workmates and found the work tolerable enough. However, she detested the stinking slurry that soaked her to the skin every day.

When she was fifteen, Nellie approached her mother with a request for more pocket money. When this was refused she

*Steel Nut and Joseph Hampton Works, Wednesbury.*

decided to look around for another job. Information on a notice board displayed on All Saints Road, sent Nellie along to the Steel Nut and Joseph Hampton Works at Wednesbury. She applied for and got a job in the factory making screws for vices. Working two machines, her day began at 7.30 a.m. and went on until 5.30 p.m., Monday to Friday and 7.30 a.m. til 1 p.m. on Saturday. She received 19s per week and her mother handed her 1s 6d pocket money.

Nellie soon became friendly with two women who worked nearby. Ginny Giles was a young married woman who lived in Tilley Street, and there was Liza Pitt, who was in her forties. The two women ran clubs and out of her 1s 6d pocket money, Nellie was expected to pay 3d per week in Bakers Shoe Club, run by Ginny. The shoes cost around 5s 11d a pair and there would be a draw to see who would receive the first pair. Another 3d went into Liza's clothing club, run for Hawkins at Walsall, which provided 'pinners' and other necessary items of clothing.

Nearly every Friday night Annie and Jim went to the pictures, leaving Nellie to look after the others. She didn't mind this, as once

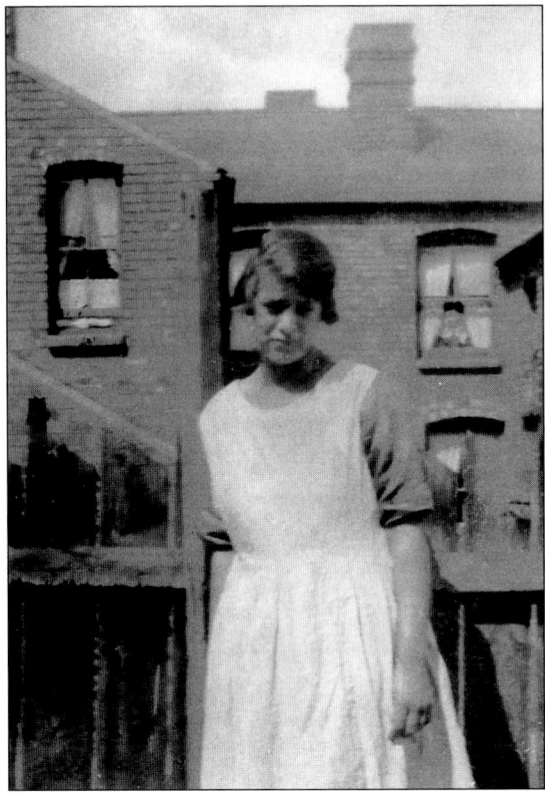

*Nellie aged fifteen.*

Tom, Evelyn and Marie were bathed and put to bed, Annie Harper and Violet usually came in to keep her company. A new hair fashion popular just then was the semi-shingle and Nellie had pleaded with Jim to let her have her waist length hair cut short. Jim's reply was emphatic, 'If thee cuts thee hair off, me wench, I'll cut thee two bloody feet off!'

Violet, however, was determined to be in the fashion. She arrived one Friday night with Annie and a bag containing a pair of sharp scissors and some curling tongs. Annie wielded the scissors with more enthusiasm than skill and soon the quarry floor was covered with Violet's dark tresses. The result, however, pleased her and much encouraged, she decided she would have her sideboards curled. The tongs were thrust into the glowing coals and when she judged them ready, Annie withdrew them and applied them carefully to Violet's hair. The cascade of curls delighted them and the cooling tongs were re-inserted into the fire to heat up, ready for the other side. While they waited the girls gossiped happily, discussing the lads of their acquaintance. Even the rather staid Nellie was beginning to display some interest in this direction, although she had not, as yet, begun to 'walk the town' with the others, which was the usual method of getting to meet the opposite sex.

Suddenly Annie recalled the job in hand. She hastily withdrew the curling irons and immediately began to wind the remaining strands of hair around them. The hair began to smoke and sizzle and, to Annie's horror, a scorched bundle of curls dropped to the floor. Violet's hand flew to her head and she wailed in dismay, 'Oh my God, me owd mon'll bloody kill me!'

The resulting mess was concealed beneath a 'Rinkie' hat, a woollen tight fitting affair with a turned-back brim and Violet wore it until the offending hair had grown to a decent length.

# 16

# Nancy

When Nellie was nearly sixteen she met Nancy Davis, who was eventually to marry her brother, George. Nance lived in Wednesbury and worked at Guest, Keen & Nettlefolds (GKN) with two of her close friends, Aggie Lunn and Floss Ellund. They would meet Nellie on the Walsall road every night when she came out of work.

Nance, a year or so older than Nellie, was a slim, vivacious girl with a sharp tongue and a wicked sense of fun. The four girls would arrange to meet every Monday night to go to the Olympia Picture House in Bell Street, usually referred to as 'The Limp'. On Tuesdays they would visit the Picturedrome ('The Drome') and on Saturday

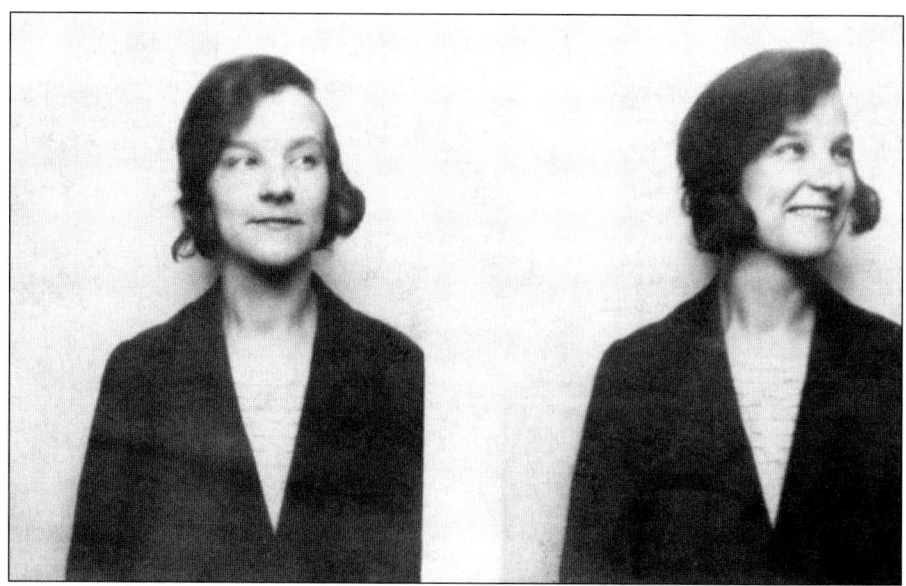

*Nancy Davis.*

night it would be 'The Limp' again. It cost 6*d* in the front seats, 9*d* in the middle and 1*s* in the posh seats at the back.

Nellie once begged Jim for sixpences to go the 'Limp' every night for a week to see *Over the Hill*. It was a very sad film and the girls 'cried their eyes up' each time they saw it.

Other nights, when Nellie was free to go out, they would meet by Bass's on the Walsall road. Sometimes Nance would say 'Let's goo an' see what owd Baggott's got.' Mr Baggott had a large yard in Birmingham Street, filled with an assortment of second-hand furniture and oddments, which he attempted to sell in his shop. The girls liked to wander around poking in drawers and turning over the rubbish, which for the most part was what it was. To arrive at the yard they would cut up through the alley, a narrow brick-paved passage at the bottom of Hill Street, which led out into Alexander Road.

At the corner of Hill Street was a large old house and whenever they ran past it up the alley, the girls would take it in turns to kick

*Nellie pictured in the alley, 1990.*

*The path to Hill Street.*

the door. On one occasion it was Aggie's turn to do the honours. 'Goo on Ag,' the others urged her. So Aggie gave the door a hefty kick but this time it was swiftly opened and the unfortunate Aggie was dragged inside and given a good 'thrairpin'.

In the meantime the others had fled, howling with merriment, which in no way abated when Aggie came panting into the yard a few minutes later, rubbing her behind.

'Pore owd Ag,' chuckled Floss, ''e must 'ave bin waitin' fer thee.'

'Ere Ag, cum an' try this cheer fer size,' called Nance. The chair she was indicating was a very old-fashioned baby's high chair and as Aggie obligingly fitted her sore bum into the seat, Nance pushed the stick, which was intended to secure the infant, across the front.

Aggie was well and truly trapped. 'I can't get the stick out,' she complained after struggling with it for several minutes.

The irrepressible Nance darted to the back door of the house and knocking loudly, she shouted, 'Mr Baggott, they'm messin' wi' yer things.' Without waiting to see what happened, Nance, Nellie and

Floss ran out of the yard, leaving poor Aggie struggling desperately to free herself. Old man Baggott came hobbling out of the back door in time to see Aggie shuffling towards the gate with the chair clamped firmly to her backside. He shook his fist at her, 'You'm a very wicked person,' he shouted and set off in pursuit. But with a last violent wrench, Aggie managed to withdraw the stick and dropping the chair with a clatter, she raced off to find the others.

It was Nance who persuaded Nellie to 'walk the town' with them, and she eventually agreed, knowing full well that there would be trouble if her dad found out. She told Jim that she was going to All Saints' Church on Sunday night before setting off to meet Nance and the others. When she got home later that night Jim asked who had been preaching, Captain Cobb or the Vicar, Lovegrove Hermann.

Mentally crossing her fingers, Nellie replied, 'It was Captain Cobb'.

'No, it weren't,' piped up Tom, who had been to church. 'It were the vicar.' As a result of her fibbing, Nellie had to stay in the following Sunday.

Another occasion when she was found out, was when she and the others had been chatting to a few lads on the Bull Stake. Suddenly Nellie reeled back from a stinging blow on her ear and, looking round she saw Jim, his face suffused with anger. 'Down the road wi' yer,' he muttered and Nellie flew.

Jim had gone as usual to hear the Salvation Army band play and Nellie had forgotten. She was waiting with some trepidation for him to come home but Jim did not strike her again, he merely said that she must not go out at all for a week.

Nance became a frequent visitor to the house in Whitton Street and after a time Nellie noticed that George was usually hanging about whenever she appeared.

He remained the quiet lad he had always been and, although rather shy, he was very fond of dancing. Dances were held regularly at the Town Hall, Charles Richard's Canteen, Lloyds Canteen and St Joseph's. Nance also enjoyed dancing and, as the pair of them often met, their friendship rapidly grew.

Nellie never mastered the art of dancing, however, and when she was sixteen George took her to Lloyds Canteen. They shuffled round the floor for a while, George instructing her in a few steps. Then the band struck up with 'Home Sweet Home', and George gave up in despair. 'Let's goo 'um, our wench,' he said, and they went.

Nance was an avid theatre-goer and, although Nellie was never really keen, preferring to go to the pictures, Nance would often persuade her to go with them to Wednesbury Theatre.

On Friday nights two could get in for the price of one, so the evening's entertainment cost 5*d* altogether and would include 3*d* for the ticket, 1*d* for a bag of rice pudding (to be eaten with a spoon brought from home) and two ½*d* slices of dip (bread soaked in meat juices). They would cry at performances of *East Lynne* and shiver and thrill to *Maria of the Red Barn*, and when the play ended at around 10.00 p.m. the girls would leave Nellie on Kings Hill and she would run home alone.

# 17

# Town Hall Dances

Annie was a staunch Conservative and she wore her Primrose badge with pride. She attended all the meetings of the Primrose League and, together with the other Conservative women, she spent a considerable amount of time canvassing for her favourite candidate.

Jim's interest in politics was tepid; he had little time for anything other than drinking, pigeon-flying and his meetings with the 'Buffs'. However, he looked upon Annie's political activities with indulgence, even allowing his front room to be hired out as a committee meeting place when the Council or General Elections were in progress.

Meetings for the opposing parties took place nearly every night for three weeks before voting day and during that time photographs of the candidates and their families were displayed in nearly every window. Nance and Nellie favoured the Primrose League while Aggie and Floss supported the Labour Party.

The girls loved to attend the meetings held in the Town Hall and would sit high up in the gallery to listen to the speakers. If he happened to be Conservative, Aggie and Floss would heckle and boo and Nellie and Nance would do likewise at a Labour Meeting. More serious-minded members of the audience would shout, 'Ave 'em out,' and the 'chuckers out' would hustle the girls towards the nearest exit.

The night before voting day ardent Conservatives were gathered outside the Town Hall before setting off on a march which would take them through Wednesbury, past the Patent Shaft and on to Tipton Conservative Club where a meeting was to be held. The marchers carried torches made of wooden sticks, wrapped in tar-soaked rags.

George said to his mother, 'Is it alright if me an' Nellie goo to Tipton wi' the procession?' and Annie, knowing that it would be at least one o'clock in the morning before they returned said, 'Ar but doe let thee dad know, I'll leave the back door open for yer.'

Brother and sister hurried up to the Town Hall and among the crowd already gathered, sought out Nance, who had arrived early and was impatient to be off.

As the darkness deepened, the torches lit up the enthusiastic faces of the marchers and the mounted policemen, who would accompany them. The crowd gradually thickened as along the way, other supporters joined to swell their ranks. Singing broke out as they swept through the town and if they happened to meet any of the opposition on the way, good natured jeers and badinage would be exchanged. The policemen, who were there ostensibly to keep order, were never called upon to use their authority.

When the meeting finally came to an end and the crowds had dispersed, George, Nellie and Nance started on the long trek home. Nance remarked wearily, 'You doe really notice the distance cummin' but it's a bloody long way to walk back 'um.'

On New Year's Eve a dance was held at the Town Hall. It was an important event and would be attended by Darlaston's gentry. George and Nance looked forward to going and George, prompted by Nance, persuaded Nellie to go with them.

Fearing that she would be left on her own when the couple were on the dance floor, Nellie suggested that she bring a friend along to make up a foursome. As there was no suitable lad available, she invited Lilly Leevesly, who lived opposite in Cope Street. Lily was a quiet wench and she and Nellie regularly attended the Wellcroft Street Chapel in Wednesbury and, as she had about as much prowess in dancing as Nellie, she would be quite happy to observe rather than participate.

The girls grew quite excited as the big day approached and talked of little else. They decided to splash out and have a new dress apiece. Six yards of identical green velvet was purchased costing 3s 11d a yard, together with a few yards of white swansdown for trimming the neck and sleeves.

Faith Horton, who lived in Station Street, was entrusted to make them up, varying the style of each one slightly. The girls also went to Underwood's shoe shop in King Street and bought a pair of black patent leather slippers, costing 6s 11d a pair. They were advised by the assistant to rub a little Vaseline into the slippers to prevent them from cracking, advice which proved to be quite useless, for when they had been worn twice, all the patent leather dropped off.

On the big night the four young people made their way to the Town Hall, Nellie and Lily very conscious of their new clothes and feeling really grand.

Strains of the dance music met them as they approached, mingling with the frosty air. The building blazed with lights and the entrance was thronged with fur-coated ladies, rubbing shoulders with cloth-covered wenches.

George and Nance took to the floor as soon as their coats had been deposited in the cloakroom. Nellie and Lily, feeling rather overawed now in the company of so many 'nobs', found seats by the wall, partially covered by the fronds of a large potted palm. There they remained for the whole of the evening, wallflowers in truth for nobody asked either of them to dance.

On the stroke of midnight the floor was cleared and one of the company, pretending to be a very old man, was ceremoniously chased out of the door while a decorated float was being dragged in. Out sprang a small girl dressed all in white with a glittering tinsel head-dress, to represent the New Year. The band then struck up with 'Auld Lang Syne' and Nellie joined hands with the others to sing the old familiar words.

# 18

# George White & 'The Pay Mon'

At nineteen years of age, Nellie had grown into a lovely young woman. Her grey eyes were clear and bright and her skin and shapely mouth required no help from cosmetics. Her hair, though thick and glossy, was unfashionably long, as most of her friends had followed Violet's example and had theirs cut into the shingle. Nellie decided she would have hers cut too and told her mother of her decision.

'You please yerself,' Annie shrugged, 'but yer know what yer dad's gonna say.'

Nellie did know, but nevertheless, she went to Snape's hair-dressing shop and soon her long dark tresses were lying at Mr Snape's feet. As she left the shop, she pulled on her Rinkie hat, hoping to conceal her shorn head for as long as possible.

Jim was sitting at the table when she returned home, having just finished his meal. Nellie hung up her jacket on a hook near the stairs and entered the kitchen still wearing the hat.

Jim greeted her cheerfully, 'Wot's the matter wi' thee 'ead me wench?' he asked. Nellie slowly pulled off her hat, looking anxiously at her father. Jim's face registered shock and disapproval and then he turned away. He said nothing and it was several days before he spoke to her again, during which time Nellie suffered more acutely than if he had beaten her.

At work, during the morning, Ginny was feeling unwell. She asked if Nellie would accompany her to the surgery and this meant a walk through the foundry. The wenches were always reluctant to walk through alone as they would be subjected to the whistles and catcalls of the men. Nellie agreed to provide moral support and they set off, trying their best to ignore the inevitable attentions they received as

*Nellie in a studio portrait.*

soon as they entered the hot, noisy machine shop. Nellie looked straight ahead as she marched along at Ginny's side but she couldn't fail to notice a young man, who stared at her in silence with unfeigned interest. Ginny nudged her as they passed him and winked at her significantly.

As they sat waiting for nurse to attend her, Ginny said, 'Did yer notice that chap?'

'Which one?' asked Nellie, knowing perfectly well.

'Yer know,' said Ginny, 'the one as was starin' at yer.'

'I never noticed 'im,' lied Nellie.

'Well 'e was,' persisted Ginny. ''Is name's George White. You 'ave a good look at 'im when we goo back.'

After work that evening, as they all walked home, Ginny glanced over her shoulder and saw George White a few paces behind. Her face lit up mischievously and she called back to him, 'Hey George, Nellie's gooin' ter Blackpool on Sunday mornin,' eleven o'clock from James Bridge station.'

'Ginny!' cried the scandalised Nellie, 'wot did yer 'ave ter tell 'im for?'

On Sunday morning Nellie arrived at the sunlit station with Jim and Tom. To her mingled surprise and embarrassment, a tall thin young man was standing on the platform, a little way off. He was smartly dressed in a navy blue suit with a white silk scarf around his neck. He carried a grey overcoat and wore a velour trilby, which he politely removed when he saw Nellie and her father descending the steps.

'Who's that?' queried Jim, seeing Nellie's blazing face.

'Oh, it's just one o' the chaps from werk,' replied Nellie.

''E must be gooin' ter Blackpool on 'is own,' observed Jim.

To Nellie's relief Tom gave a shout and pointed to the train, which had just appeared in the distance in a billow of white smoke. Her relief was short-lived, however, as George followed them into the nearest carriage. On the journey to Blackpool, George and her father became engaged in easy conversation but Nellie said little and seemed particularly absorbed in the swiftly passing scenery. When the train arrived at Blackpool and the passengers alighted, George stood there awkwardly, twisting the brim of his hat round and round. Jim drew Nellie aside and whispered, 'Why doe yer ask that young fellow if he wants ter cum wi' we. It's a shame if 'e 'as ter spend the day on 'is own.'

Nellie, who had not been entirely as disinterested as she pretended to be, nodded her head and shyly approached the young man. 'Me Dad says would yer like ter cum wi' we?' she asked. The grateful look which flashed into his eyes made Nellie's knees tremble a little and they smiled at each other for the first time. They walked along the promenade together until Jim, with a twinkle in his eye stopped and said, 'I think I'll tek Tum fer a paddle, 'e's never sin the sea before.' Neither had Nellie, but Jim suggested that she and George have a look round the town and then all meet later at the station. Without any reluctance whatsoever Nellie said, 'Ta-ra' to her father and brother and the young couple wandered off together.

George suggested that they should first go to the tower to hear the orchestra play. Nellie readily agreed and as they made their way to the famous landmark, she told George that her father had once done some work on the tower many years ago.

As they entered the ballroom, the orchestra was playing *Cavalleria Rusticana*. 'I play that on me violin,' George said, steering Nellie towards the nearest empty seats. ''Ow long 'ave you bin playin'?' asked Nellie.

'Since I was little,' he replied. 'Me mother can play as well an' I suppose I learnt a lot of it from 'er. I play sometimes at the dances at the Catholic School,' he added.

At the end of a very pleasant day they returned to the station and, on the journey home, George sat himself down beside Nellie, under the amused scrutiny of her father. Tom, replete with food and fresh air, slept soundly, waking only when shaken by Jim as the train pulled into James Bridge station.

George walked in silence at Nellie's side until they reached Whitton Street. Goodnights were said and he departed, pausing to wave his hat before Nellie and others plunged into the darkness of the entry.

'He's a nice chap,' Jim commented. 'Thee wants ter 'ang on ter 'im, me wench.'

'I doe know wot mek's yer think I want ter 'ang onto 'im,' she retorted. 'I doe want ter goo courtin' anybody yet.'

During the weeks that followed, Nellie went out of her way to avoid George. She admitted to herself that she liked him but she was unwilling to make a commitment of any kind.

George was patient, however, and persisted in hanging around at the top of Whitton Street for hours, in the hope that Nellie would appear.

'That chap's waitin' at the top o' the street agen,' Tom announced one tea-time.

'Which chap?' Annie wanted to know.

'Oh, he's just somebody as werks at our place,' said Nellie, blushing in spite of herself.

'Well why doe yer goo an' see 'im if 'e's waitin' fer you,' said Annie. 'Is 'e the one yer dad told me about as went ter Blackpool wi' yer?'

'That's 'im,' replied Tom promptly, before Nellie could reply.

'I thought you was gooin' up the Limp,' said Annie presently, as Nellie sat down by the fire with some crochet work.

'I was,' she replied, 'but I doe think I'll bother now. I was gooin' on me own any road.'

'Well if it's 'cause o' that chap, you con always climb over the fence round the back an' goo up that way. You said yer dayn't want ter miss that picture.'

'I did want ter see it,' admitted Nellie. 'I suppose I may as well goo now I've got meself ready.'

'I think you'm bein' daft anyway,' sniffed Annie. 'If yer doe want ter see 'im, why doe yer just tell 'im?'

As soon as she had gone, Tom sped down the entry and up the street. George was still there, leaning against Cresswell's shop window with his hands in his pockets.

*Cresswell's shop.*

'Am yer waitin' fer our Nellie?' Tom asked him.

George just smiled and shook his head. 'Well just in case you wos,' Tom informed him, 'her's gone ter the Limp.'

George straightened up smartly. ''Ow long agoo,' he asked.

Tom grinned, 'About five minutes agoo. If you 'urry up you might catch 'er up.' George nodded and walked quickly away, breaking into a run as soon as he got round the corner.

Nellie had just settled into her seat as the lights were dimming, when George slid into the seat beside her. It had been easy for him to locate her as most of the seats were empty.

She turned her head and smiled shyly at him, experiencing again that odd mixture of pleasure and reluctance each time she saw him.

'Why did yer goo the back way?' he whispered, bending his head close to hers. When Nellie said nothing, he continued, 'You don't 'ave to avoid me, yer know. If yer don't want to see me, just say so.' Her heart fluttered queerly at his direct words. She turned her head and looked at him. 'I doe know what I want,' she said softly. 'I've never 'ad a chap before.'

George's hand closed over hers, 'Well you've got one now, Nell,' he grinned.

She continued to see him only occasionally however, and their meetings were always contrived by George, who would stand at his attic window to practise his violin and watch for her to pass by on her way to the 'Limp'. Shortly afterwards he would slip into the seat beside her and later walk her home.

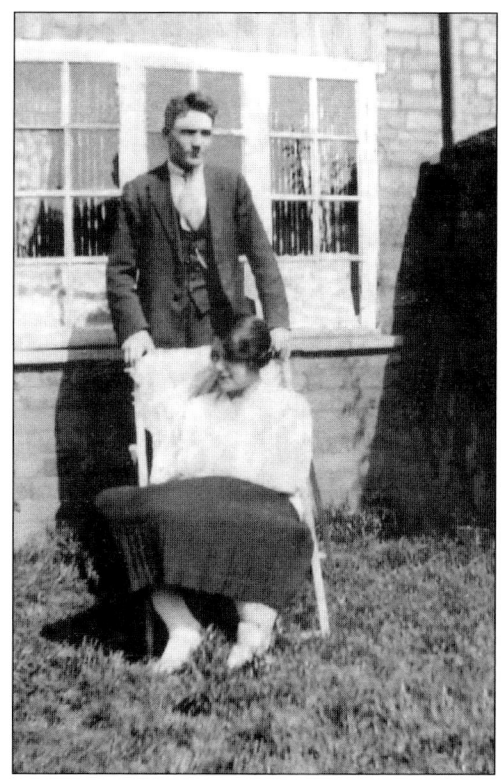

*Nellie and George at the time when they were courting.*

Nellie was teased unmercifully by her workmates, who did their best to encourage the courtship.

'I 'ear you'm gooin' wi' the paymon's son,' said a woman, who worked at a machine nearby.

'Who der yer mean?' asked Nellie puzzled. 'Who's the pay mon?'

'Yer know, George White's feyther. He used ter sell chips an' pays from a barrer round the streets an' 'is mother keeps a little shop in Church Street.'

Nellie knew all about the shop for she had passed it many times, but she had never met Mrs White and knew little or nothing about the family.

She asked her mother about the 'pay mon' and Annie said she remembered him well as he had been a well-known figure around Darlaston and the delicious chips and peas cooked by Mrs White were always in much demand.

About the man himself, Annie said, there had been some sort of scandal but he had been dead for some time.

'What sort of scandal?' asked Nellie. Her mother pursed her lips together.

'I think you'd best ask George about 'im,' she replied. 'I doe really remember what 'append.'

'Tell me,' Nellie persisted. 'You must know somethin', an it can't be much of a secret if folks knows about it.'

'Well', said Annie reluctantly, 'I 'eard as he'd attacked a policeman an' spent years in jail.'

'THE PAY MON'
Edward White was born in The Green, Darlaston, on 16 January 1861. The events of his life can be traced mainly through police records, for he spent most of it in prison.

At the age of eleven, or at least not later than 1872, Edward claims to have enlisted in the 2nd Battalion Lincolnshire 10th Regiment and, according to his Police Service Record, he served for six years, two hundred and ninety three days. At the age of eighteen or no later than 1879, it appears that he began a prison sentence for an offence committed while serving in the army and he was transferred to Broadmoor Hospital two years later.

On Edward's later evidence given at Stafford Assizes in 1903, he was released from Broadmoor in 1885 aged twenty-four. However, Broadmoor has no record of his having been there during this time.

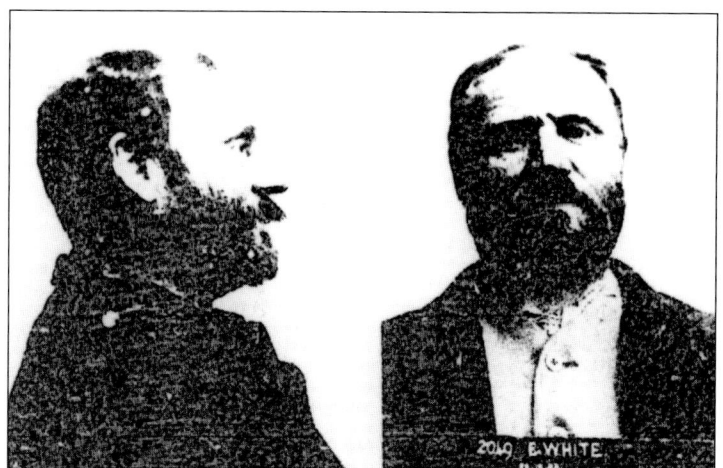

*Edward
White.*

The subsequent period of his life has been verified by well-documented sources and confirms that on 1 February 1886, aged twenty-four years and eleven months, Edward enlisted in the Staffordshire Constabulary. His description at this time is of a man whose height was 5ft 10in, eyes blue, hair light brown, complexion fair, and it was also recorded that he was a miner by trade.

On 1 April 1886 he was appointed constable and stationed at Darlaston, but on 29 May of the following month he was dismissed for being drunk on duty. On 15 November of the same year he married Martha Bird, and from the inscription in a bible given to Martha by her sister Caroline, it is clear that the couple emigrated to America in April 1887. They travelled steerage, cooking their meals on deck, and arrived in the New World to complete the remainder of the journey to Pittsburgh. It was here in 1891 that Charlie was born; it was also the year of their return to England.

The family settled again in Darlaston in a small house in New Street. In this house on 15 June 1893 a second son Albert was born, followed on 27 September 1895 by the birth of a daughter christened Martha after her mother.

Edward was again in trouble with the police when in June 1896, he was found guilty of being drunk and disorderly and was fined twenty shillings plus costs; he was described at this period as being a hawker. A more serious offence occurred on the night of 31 October 1896 when Edward attacked PC Birchall in Church Street. On

10 November he was committed to the Stafford Assizes and consequently transferred to Broadmoor on 22 February 1897 to serve a seven-year prison sentence. He spent most of his time during his stay doing sums and helping on the wards. He was transferred to Portland prison on 13 December 1900, remaining for four months where he completed his sentence. He returned to his former place of residence in Staffordshire and began a business in the fish line. He did well, gaining employment as a boat measurer earning 27s a week.

Upon his release in 1903, the family moved to Catherine's Cross but before long Edward was in trouble again. On 10 August in the same year, PC Louis Sebastian Marshall saw him appear from behind a wall near Jones's pawn shop. Edward was apparently agitated and possibly drunk. He asked the constable to accompany him home for, he said, he was afraid of his wife who, he added, was sure to cut his throat. PC Marshall told him to go home and not talk nonsense and it seems that Edward was persuaded. Shortly afterwards, however, he appeared again, this time attacking the policeman with a shovel causing injury to his arm. Edward was arrested and committed to take his trial at the next Assizes to be held at Stafford.

On 7 December 1903, Edward was charged with grievous bodily harm and found guilty though not responsible for his actions. He was sentenced to be detained at His Majesty's pleasure in Broadmoor Hospital. On 11 December, George was born. During his time at Broadmoor he studied arithmetic, he read and painted with watercolours and he also helped as a ward cleaner. In 1913, when he was fifty-two years old, Edward wrote a letter from Rampton Hospital, dated 27 September. It contained the following poem, dedicated to his wife:

> If I have caused you grief or pain
> Or one pulsate of heart,
> You only have to mention it
> To stab me like a dart.
> For I am sensitive to all
> You have to say,
> And like a snail sprinkled with salt
> I dwindle right away.

I think of you my darling wife
And heartily I pray,
For God to send you happiness,
And comfort every day.
For you have worked most nobly
As everybody knows,
Until your cheeks are sunken in
And bones show through your clothes.

Your chest is flat and sunken in
And shoulders up and round,
And astupe so awkwardly
That you look at the ground.
With toes pent in and heels turned out
You waddle with a gait,
Just like a duck with pattens on
Or a toad that's lost its mate.

I could have wept aloud with joy
The day that you were here.
To dandle Georgie on my knee
And o'er him drop a tear.
But, to have done so, understand
When we were doomed to part,
Would have grieved me very much
If not have broke my heart.

The pair of roses you brought here
Look elegant and grand,
I know they've love within their hearts
By the shaking of their hand.
They tell me they will come again,
Most like at Sheffield Fair,
With Joe and Edith, May and June
To scatter my despair.

*White's shop.*

On 24 May 1914, Edward was conditionally discharged to the Salvation Army aged fifty-four. Back in Darlaston again, he returned to Martha and 26 Church Street. It was during this time that he became known as the 'Pay Mon', selling fish, chips and peas that Martha cooked from a small red painted cart. He would also be remembered for the little tin photographs that he took on Sunday afternoons. Life with Martha proved to be as disastrous as before and in 1924 he moved to number 13 Bell Street, just a short distance away from the little shop, to live with his son Charlie and wife Nancy.

*Above: No. 13
Bell Street.*

*Edward White's
grave in James
Bridge Cemetery.*

A grave in James Bridge Cemetery, bordered with old blue bricks, bears no name and no headstone, but the old 'Pay Mon' lies there with Charlie and Nancy. He died on 14 February 1926, aged sixty-five.

# 19

# Loss

Her mother's disclosures about George's father made no difference at all to Nellie and she continued to see him occasionally. Annie Harper and Violet were both courting so Nellie saw little of them now, but Lily was a frequent companion and she also saw a great deal of Nance, whose romance with her brother was progressing nicely. The old Saturday night traditional get-together with her relatives had been resumed after the war and hilarious evenings were spent at the house in Whitton Street.

A piano, which Jim had bought from Taylor's in Walsall, now had pride of place in Annie's front room. No-one in the family knew how to play it, but Billy Wilmore, who was Captain of the Darlaston Fire Brigade, was often prevailed upon to provide accompaniment to all the old songs.

To celebrate Jim's birthday Annie had ordered a barrel of beer and all the family and neighbours were invited in. The front door was opened wide to the street and anyone passing could help themselves to a pork sandwich and beer, which flowed freely. It flowed over the table too, soaking Annie's cloth and ran onto the floor, later to be swept out of the front door.

But for the family these happy times were soon to end and the fabric of their lives torn and damaged beyond repair.

Jim came home early from work and sat down heavily in his chair. 'Doe get me any dinner me wench.' he said. 'I doe feel like anythin' to eat at all.'

'Why, wot's the matta?' asked Annie. 'Aint yer very well?'

'I 'ad a bit of an accident this mornin' an' it's left me a bit sick,' Jim explained. He explained how he and his mate had been breaking concrete to lay a machine. The other chap had let go his end of the heavy iron bar they'd been carrying and it had struck Jim in the stomach.

Annie put down the teapot and looked at her husband anxiously, 'Do yer think yer should goo an' see the doctor, Jim?' she asked.

'No,' he replied shaking his head. 'I'll be all right just now, doe worry yerself.'

He returned to work the next day, insisting that he was all right, but as the weeks went by it became obvious to Annie that he was having frequent bouts of pain, although he did his best to conceal it from her. In the end she insisted that he should see the doctor and to her relief, Jim agreed.

Dr Magrane diagnosed gallstones and said he would make arrangements for Jim to have a further examination at the Royal Hospital, Wolverhampton. There was a period of waiting before a letter arrived requesting Jim to attend the hospital the next day. He was admitted shortly afterwards and underwent an operation. Dr Magrane's diagnosis had been incorrect, but cancer was a dreaded word that was never mentioned, or if it was, spoken of in whispers, and as far as the rest of the family and friends were concerned, the cause of Jim's illness remained a mystery.

The operation was followed by sixteen weeks in hospital, during which time Annie and the family visited every day. Nellie had no time for George White, for every evening after work she would hurry home and, after a quick bite to eat, she caught the tram on the Bull Stake to Wolverhampton.

On Sunday 26 September 1926, she was returning from the hospital with Annie and George, when Annie suddenly exclaimed that she had forgotten to get Jim's State Note from the sister. Nellie and George caught the next tram back to Wolverhampton, and when they obtained the note, they walked around the corner of the huge hospital building to Vicarage Road. Looking up, they could just see Jim on the balcony. He was sitting in a chair with a blanket around his shoulders, enjoying the balmy September evening.

Nellie shouted and waved and Jim's face lit up with a smile when he saw them. 'Tell yer mother I'll soon be 'ome,' he called.

Brother and sister waved once more before setting off home. It was the last time they saw their father alive.

They had only just reached the door when a policeman arrived with an urgent message from the hospital. Annie, much agitated, returned to the Royal with Nellie and George. They were met with the news that Jim had choked to death, following a severe attack of coughing.

He was just forty-six years old and Annie could not accept that their life together had ended. Grief wrapped itself around her like a blanket and she was blind to everything but her sorrow. Although he had been absent from the house for many weeks, while Jim lived a sense of his presence had remained in the house. But it seemed now that he was dead, the presence had departed too, leaving behind a family bereft of the warm and stabilising influence.

Annie and the younger children expressed their sorrow in stormy tears and with the crying had come some measure of relief. For Nellie and George however, more reserved and self-contained than the others, the loss of their beloved father had bitten too deeply to be washed away easily and they went about with burning eyes and sore, tight throats.

As soon as he learned of Jim's death, George White called to see Annie, to express his sympathy and ask if there was any help he could give them.

Annie invited the young man in and he shyly entered the house for the first time. Nellie spoke little but her mother told George the details of her husband's death and the arrangements that were being made for the funeral.

When he had drunk the tea, which Nellie had made for him, he stood up and thanked her, repeating his offer of help to her mother. Annie was impressed by his sincerity and politeness and she invited him to attend the funeral and to call at the house whenever he wished.

Nellie walked with him to the entry and as they stood in the darkness, George reached for her hand. 'I'm really sorry about yer dad, Nell,' he said quietly. 'I know how much you must 'ave thought of him.'

'Nobody knows,' muttered Nellie and she broke down and sobbed her heart out. George held her closely and when the tears had subsided he gently wiped her face with his handkerchief.

'Can I come again, Nell?' he pleaded. 'Will I really be welcome?'

Nellie lifted her head and even in the darkness, she could feel the intensity of his look. She knew at last that to deny her feelings for him would be stupid and senseless. It suddenly occurred to her that the love she had just lost with the death of her father was now being offered to her again, a hundredfold, and she knew that she would regret it to her dying day if she did not accept it.

Her answer to him was not in words but when they parted a little while later, they both knew that whatever joy or grief the future held in store for them, they would share it together.

## 20

# Goodbye Jim

The night before the funeral, Jim's body was brought home. The solemn-faced men from Webbs carried the coffin into the front room and placed it upon two chairs. The coffin lid was removed so that the family could gaze once more upon the beloved features. As she looked down upon the dead face she had loved so much, Annie thought how peaceful Jim looked. The lines of suffering had been wiped away and he looked younger than when she had seen him on her last visit to the hospital. Her eyes took in every detail of the lace-trimmed shroud and the white satin lining of the coffin, puckered into tiny bunches of forget-me-nots.

She put out a loving hand to stroke the black, crinkly hair and her fingers touched the cold face, tracing its contours. Nellie, barely able to contain the grief, which had once more welled up inside her as she watched her mother's last caresses, knelt down on the floor beside the coffin and placed her warm hand on the cold stiff hands of her father. George and Tom knelt down beside her with bowed heads, fighting back the tears, while Evelyn and Marie clung tearfully to their mother.

Kindly neighbours came in to offer comfort to the bereaved family and Jim's brothers and their wives arrived to give their support.

The funeral took place on Friday 1 October. The days following Jim's death had passed in a kind of daze for Annie but with the help of family and neighbours, the catering had been organised, and she and the children were fitted out with heavy black mourning clothes, even having white handkerchiefs with a black border.

Annie had wanted no expense spared for his funeral and three cabs had been ordered for the cortège. The glass hearse was drawn by four black horses wearing jet-black plumes, and was followed by the first cab pulled by two horses. Two steps led into the interior, which had darkened glass windows and seats on either side to accommodate three people.

Annie had been overwhelmed by the masses of flowers which had been arriving at the house and by the number of folks who had called to pay their last respects.

Before setting out for the service at All Saints' Church, the guests were offered a glass of port and a thin arrowroot biscuit. One or two neighbours remained behind to put the finishing touches to the cold spread of cooked meats, fruit and seed cake.

Annie bore up well during the service, her sobs muffled behind the heavy veil, as the vicar addressed the packed congregation. Jim Askey had been a popular and well-respected man and the number of people who attended the funeral bore testimony to this. Among those present, clad for the most part in sober black or dark attire, the full regalia of Jim's fellow Buffs stood out sharply in contrast. When the procession arrived at James Bridge Cemetery they lifted the coffin onto their shoulders and carried it slowly to the graveside. A few members of their order had previously visited the cemetery and they had lined the grave with ivy leaves. Nellie stood at her mother's side as the vicar intoned the final words. Annie's sobs grew louder as the moment came for her to sprinkle earth onto the coffin. Nellie tried to take her mother's arm but Annie was oblivious to the gesture and sank to her knees beside the grave. Then Cal came forward and gently but firmly pulled her to her feet and led her away.

Nellie felt a comforting arm about her shoulders and she looked with tear-blinded eyes into the face of George White, who smiled reassuringly at her as they slowly walked away towards the cemetery gates.

During the weeks following the funeral, Annie refused to be left alone. George and Nellie spent miserable evenings listening to her endless moans and rantings. She was filled now with self-pity and resented bitterly that she had been left to face life alone. Nellie tried to dissuade George from coming to the house so often, but he refused to listen saying that if they could not go out alone together, he would prefer to stay in, even to humour her mother.

Occasionally Nance and Nellie's brother, George, would take Annie to the theatre and they were able to go to the pictures by themselves.

Nellie's love for George grew stronger as time went on. He was unfailingly polite and considerate to her mother and, although he rarely spoke of his home life, Nellie knew that he was often unhappy, and her heart ached for him.

Her brother, George, approved of their relationship and found that he had much in common with the quiet, serious young man.

Tom, seemingly unaffected by their recent loss, had soon regained his buoyant manner and his cheery demeanour helped to bring a little life back into the house. He regarded Nellie's young man as being a bit too quiet, but he liked him well enough. Evelyn and Marie looked forward to George's visit as he would occasionally bring them some little treat from his mother's shop.

One rainy Saturday night the couple were returning from a visit to the pictures at Walsall. The tram was full inside so they were obliged to sit on the open top, which offered no shelter from the elements. George turned up the collar of his coat and glanced at Nellie's uncovered head, which was fast becoming soaked in the pouring rain.

'This is no good, Nell,' he said, wiping away little rivulets from his face, 'I can't see the sense in this traipsin' about. We may as well get married.'

Nellie looked up somewhat startled. 'I doe know, George,' she replied. 'I 'adn't really thought about it.'

'Well think about it then,' he smiled, 'an' let me know what you decide termorra.'

# 21

# Marriage

George arrived at the house the following night and addressing Annie, he came straight to the point. "As Nell towd yer wot I asked 'er last night?' Nellie shot him a warning glance; her mother was not in the best of moods, but George would not be put off.

'I asked 'er ter marry me,' he announced.

Annie's face was a study as she looked from one to the other, but she remained silent.

"Ow do we goo about puttin' the banns in?' he asked her unperturbed.

'Yowd betta goo an' find out!' Annie retorted, and she would say nothing further on the subject.

'It's not as her don't like yer,' Nellie explained to George later. "Er just doe want ter lose me money, that's all.'

George listened grimly, determined that the wedding would go ahead as soon as the arrangements could be made, in spite of Annie's opposition.

They went together to St Lawrence's Church, often referred to as the 'Old Church'. Arrangements were made for the banns to be read and the wedding to take place in seven weeks' time on the 27 May, which would be Whit Sunday.

It was obvious that they would have to live with George's mother and it was with a great deal of trepidation that Nellie set off to visit Martha White for the first time.

Within a few minutes' conversation, Nellie's heart sank like a stone. It was quite apparent that it would be no easy task for her to live with this woman.

Mrs White looked at her future daughter-in-law with dark, suspicious eyes and her manner was disagreeable. Nellie was greatly relieved when the visit came to an end and they escaped from the dismal little room at the back of the shop. George was very quiet, as though he were afraid to ask what she thought about his mother. 'It woe be fer long, Nell,' he told her presently. 'As soon as we can, we'll ger a place of our own, I promise you.'

'It's awlright,' she assured him, 'we'll manage somehow, although I doe think yer mother likes me very much.'

'Doe talk daft,' he said, ''er aint 'ad time ter get ter know yer yet.'

That was true, thought Nellie, but if 'er thinks the same o' me as I think of 'er, it'll be a case of out o' the fryin' pan, inter the fire!

Nellie was discussing her plans with Nance. 'Wot shall yer wear?' asked Nance.

'I dunno, just a frock an' 'at, I suppose,' shrugged Nellie.

'I know somebody as will mek it fer yer,' offered Nance. ''Er name's Mrs Moseley an' 'er lives in Alexander Road. Will yer be 'avin' any flowers?'

'No,' said Nellie shaking her head, 'I probably won't bother, seein' as there's only gonna be four of we there.'

On the whole, Nance seemed to be the more excited of the two and, fired with enthusiasm, she accompanied Nellie to buy the material for the wedding dress and help choose the accessories. Three yards of blue crêpe de chine were purchased at $3s$ $11d$ a yard from the warehouse and Nellie bought a picture hat, costing $6s$ $11d$ from Cox Street. Her shoes were champagne-coloured leather from Bakers, paid for with a cheque from Ginny's shoe club.

Nance had been right to recommend Mrs Moseley, for the finished dress was exquisite, having the most intricate smocking embroidered with tiny forget-me-nots on the bodice.

Annie took no interest whatsoever in the preparations; indeed she ignored Nellie and George entirely, although eaten up inside with spite and resentment.

She held her tongue until she heard Nellie telling her brothers and sisters that George's brother, Charlie, had offered them his Rolls-Royce for the wedding and that his sister, Martha, who lived in Erdington, was arranging a small reception for the couple at her house.

Annie's anger erupted; her face distorted with malice, she poured out vituperation, threatening to go to the church and cause a disturbance. Nellie's face grew pale and her lips trembled at her mother's outburst. Her brother, George, had sat listening in silence, his mouth tightening into a hard line, until suddenly he banged with his fist on the table, making the plates jump.

'Shut yer row,' he shouted. 'I'm warnin' yer,' he said, thrusting his face close to Annie's, 'so sure as yer goo near that church I'll 'ave the bloody police waitin' fer yer. Her's gerrin married and there's no need fer 'er ter get married; you'd 'ave summat ter shout about if her was in trouble.'

After this Annie held her tongue but during the weeks preceding the wedding, Nellie's surface pleasure in her pretty things was overshadowed. Not even Nance's merry chatter or George's devotion could dispel the cloud that seemed to overhang everything.

George took her to Edwards Jewellers the following week to buy the ring. Mr Bedworth, who was an old friend of Annie's, asked George which carat he preferred.

'You can have 9, 18, or 22 carat', he explained.

'We'll 'ave 22 carat then,' said George decidedly. 'We'm only gerrin' married once.'

The ring cost £2 10s and George pocketed it carefully as they left the shop.

Nellie was awake early on her wedding day for the ceremony was to be at nine o'clock. While Evelyn and Marie were still sleeping, she slipped out of bed and crept to the window. It was going to be a lovely day, she observed with satisfaction. The sun was just appearing behind the rooftops of the close-packed little houses and the sky held a bright warm promise. She glanced about the room she had shared with her sisters for so many years and in which, after today, she would sleep no more. It must be about six o'clock she thought and began to search around the lino-covered floor for her shoes. She took an old coat from the wardrobe and slipped her arms into the sleeves, pausing as she did so to gaze lovingly at her wedding dress, the most beautiful thing she had ever possessed. She touched it gently with her fingers, stroking its generous folds. In three hours' time she would be leaving this house and her mother for good. Trying to feel some regret, she could not, her only sorrow today was that her father would not be there to see her and share in her happiness.

Tears sprang into her eyes as she thought of him, she needed him so badly today and how perfect it would have been if only he had been giving her away instead of her brother, walking into the church on his arm, supporting her with his love.

She wiped her tears away determinedly. 'No way to carry on, on your wedding day,' she told herself, and closing the bedroom door gently behind her, she made her way downstairs.

George had spent much of the previous afternoon helping his brother to polish the Rolls-Royce and when it drew up at Nellie's door it gleamed magnificently in the morning sunlight.

Nellie was relieved to see that Charlie was wearing a collar and tie instead of his habitual muffler, and that he wore shoes instead of hob-nail boots.

In the cool dark interior of St Lawrence's the vicar's solemn tones reverberated around the almost-empty church, as he read out the words of the marriage service. Nellie made her responses in a low voice, but when asked if he would take this woman for his wedded wife, George answered loudly, 'Ar, three bags full.'

Nance and George departed for Erdington as soon as the service was over. Charlie, having removed the stiff collar and replaced it with his muffler, took the newly married couple on a tour of Willenhall, Darlaston and Bilston, before setting off for Martha's.

*Nellie's wedding day.*

Nellie was extremely grateful to George's sister for the trouble she had taken in preparing the food, which included a magnificent iced cake. She was still a little in awe of this tall, rather intimidating woman, whom she had met only once or twice before, during her courtship. Martha was a sister at Highfield House, Erdington, and Nellie could easily imagine how she must put the fear of God into the young nurses under her supervision. Nevertheless, she now warmed to her new sister-in-law, who had done her best to turn her wedding day into a memorable occasion.

George's mother, who had refused to attend the wedding, was in bed, when they returned and the little house was in darkness. George remained downstairs, while Nellie made her way to the little bedroom. She lit the oil lamp, which stood on the shelf of the iron fireplace. The yellow light flickered on the walls of the tiny room and Nellie glanced around happily. Although they had very little money, she and George had worked hard to make it pretty and comfortable.

They had hung fresh wallpaper with blue flowers on a cream background and had bought a new mattress and bedsteads for £3 10*s* from Bishop Marston's. Using George's savings they had purchased a bedroom suite for nine guineas, indeed it had taken his entire savings to buy the suite and a small carpet square. Left with only one week's wages Nellie was nevertheless satisfied with the result.

It wouldn't be so bad, she thought, maybe once we've settled in Mrs White would learn to accept her. She smiled to herself as it had just occurred to her that now she too was Mrs White and she began to view the future with slightly more optimism. It would be best to forget the unhappiness of the past and look forward to a new life. Both she and George were earning, so they should be able to manage quite comfortably. She would save up and buy pretty material to make new curtains and covers for the rather drab kitchen and she would do her best to get on with George's mother.

As she undressed and put on her nightgown, a rare feeling of contentment enveloped Nellie. Then she heard her husband's tread upon the stairs, and she smiled, quite confident that at last it seemed the future had much to offer her.

# 22

# Albert James (Joe)

Nellie's hopes were short-lived. Although she and George were happy together, his mother went out of her way to make them miserable. The new curtains and covers, which Nellie had saved for and spent much time in making, had been hung one morning before she went to work. Upon her return she found that they had been removed and the old ones hung in their place.

Her mother-in-law looked at her disagreeably. 'This is my house,' she said sourly, 'an' these am my things, if yer doe like it yer know wot yer con do.'

Two weeks after she was married, Nellie had a bilious turn at work. Ginny took her to the lavatories, while Liza fetched a Setler's powder. The two women looked at each other with amusement.

'Know wot's up wi' 'er, Ginny?' asked Liza. 'Ar,' replied Ginny 'I reckon as 'er's pregnant.' Nellie looked at them in amazement. 'I can't be,' she protested, 'I've only been married fer two weeks.'

'I doe care 'ow long thist bin married, me wench. I tell thee, thist gonna 'ave a babby,' asserted Liza.

Nellie walked home with George after work.

'I 'ad a bilious tern this mornin',' she told him, 'an' yer know what Liza Pitt said?'

'What?' asked George.

''Er says I'm gonna 'ave a baby,' said Nellie.

'Could've towd thee that,' laughed George.

'What's yer mother gonna say?' asked Nellie in some dismay.

''Er con say what 'er likes,' said George firmly, 'it's got nuthin' ter do wi' 'er.'

Mrs White received the news of Nellie's pregnancy in stony silence, offering neither congratulations nor commiserations, and George believed that his mother had accepted the situation. However, as soon as she was alone with Nellie, she did her best to persuade her to get rid of the baby, suggesting various methods of making this possible. Nellie was upset, and feeling the need to talk to another woman about it, she went to see her mother for the first time since her marriage.

Annie welcomed her with some reservation but when Nellie broke down and wept and told her of the expected baby and her mother-in-law's attitude, Annie was filled with indignation.

'The bloody ole witch,' she swore. 'I've 'ad seven an' not once did I ever think o' gerrin' rid o' one. I'll tell thee wot,' she added, 'if 'er woe let thee 'ave it theer, thee cost bring it 'ere an' we'll 'ave it.' She made Nellie a cup of tea and for the first time, Nellie saw in her mother a possible ally.

The two women talked together and Nellie poured out her troubles, telling Annie how miserable and unwelcome George's mother made her feel. ''Er pokes the fire out every night at nine o'clock an' 'er won't let me wash the floor over every day, 'er says it meks the place damp,' sniffed Nellie. 'We 'ave ter ask 'er if we can goo ter the pictures or else 'er locks the door.'

Annie was sympathetic; she was pleased about the baby and was quite prepared to welcome it. 'I should tell George wot 'er said about gerrin' rid of it,' she advised. 'It's as well 'e knows wot's gooin' on.'

George was shocked and angry when Nellie told him, and he turned on his mother in a fury, leaving her in no doubt as to what he thought about her and her suggestions. She never referred to the coming baby again, but was, if anything, more disagreeable than before.

Nellie continued to work until she was seven months pregnant, managing to operate two heavy machines. The winter of 1929 was long and hard and on the freezing cold morning of 19 February, George departed for work as usual, leaving Nellie shivering in bed. It was still very early, around six o'clock, when things began to happen. Nellie, uncertain and ignorant, confessed to her mother-in-law that she had just had a 'show'. Martha's answer was brusque and unhelpful, 'Oh, it's nuthin',' she muttered, 'tek no notice.'

Nellie cleaned their room and later trudged up to the town to do some shopping. By mid-day, the pains in her back and stomach were becoming increasingly severe and she hesitatingly told Martha of her plight.

'Oh, you'll get a lot wuss before yer ger any better,' was the unsympathetic reply. To Nellie's surprise her mother-in-law began to tidy herself in preparation for a visit to her sister. As this was Wednesday and Martha's visits always took place on Thursdays, it was obvious that she intended to leave Nellie to struggle on alone.

She walked the house all that long afternoon and at half past five, she dragged herself upstairs, and lay huddled on the bed, gasping with pain at each contraction. The water broke suddenly and with its onrush, Nellie became engulfed in fear and she burst into tears.

Martha had returned, but made no effort to investigate the noises from above. When George returned at 7.00 p.m., and asked where Nellie was, she just pointed to the ceiling and shrugged.

George raced upstairs and was appalled at the state Nellie was in. 'Fetch me mother quick,' she moaned, 'an' you'd better get the midwife.'

George leapt onto his bike and pedalled furiously towards Bull Piece.

Annie's first question was, ''Ow long 'ave yer bin like this?'

'All day,' Nellie sobbed.

'You bloody ole cat!' Annie ranted at Martha. 'If 'er loses this baby, I'll swing fer yer.'

Nurse Chattaway added her imprecations to Annie's, but Martha seemed unconcerned and unrepentant.

A 7lb 3oz baby boy was born at five minutes to twelve and, even to his exhausted mother's eyes, he seemed unusually red and wrinkled.

'Don't worry,' laughed the nurse, 'they all look like that. He'll be different in a day or two.'

Nellie's first visitor the next day was her brother, Tom. Martha answered the door to him, but when he asked if he could see Nellie and his new nephew, she firmly refused.

'I'm 'avin' no men in the bedroom,' she told Tom. 'It's just not proper.'

'But I'm 'er brother,' he protested.

'I doe care if thee bist the King of England, thee bistn't gooin' up them stairs.'

When Nance saw the baby she exclaimed, 'Ooh Nell, 'e is a funny little bugger!'

Annie came frequently and made a great fuss of the baby, but Martha showed absolutely no interest in her new grandson and her indifference hurt Nellie intensely.

*George, baby Joe and Nellie.*

The baby was christened Albert James when he was three weeks old, but from the very first he was called Joe. By the time he was four months old, his father was on the dole and his mother went back to her old job at the Steel Nut.

George looked after Joe in the mornings, Nellie having washed, dressed and fed him before she left for work. At dinner time she took him to her mother's and collected him on her way home from work. She paid Annie five shillings a week for minding him. If her mother had been baking that day, she would give Nellie some cakes to share with George. Since Nellie had started back to work, Martha had cooked an evening meal for him. After a time it began to irk Nellie that as soon as she arrived home from work, a hot meal was placed before George, while all she had to eat was bread and lard. In no doubt that Martha did this to spite her, Nellie arrived home one night tired, cold and hungry. She put on the table a few small cakes her mother had made. George looked up from his plate of fish and chips. 'Wot's up, Nell?' he asked, noticing the look on her face.

'I'll tell thee wot's up,' shouted Nellie angrily. ''Ow would you like to cum 'ome from work to bread an' lard an' watch me eatin' fish an' chips. Yer mother does it on purpose. 'Er waits fer me ter cum in before 'er cooks it. I'll tell thee summat else as well. Everythin' me mother gies me, I share it wi' thee.' She sat down at the table and wept into her hands. George was aghast. He put down his knife and fork and put his hand on Nellie's arm. 'I just day think,' he said miserably, pushing his plate away. 'But I'll tell thee summat, Nell, I'll never eat anything' else off 'er.'

The incident was soon forgotten but George kept his word and refused to eat anything unless Nellie shared it.

As times became increasingly hard, for George was entitled to draw dole money for himself and Joe only, not once did they reveal to anyone how little they had. Ginny and Liza soon began to realise, however, when they noticed that from Wednesday, when the money was gone, until Friday, Nellie's lunch consisted of two slices of dry toast a day. Things began to get even worse, and Nellie was reduced to making up a feed from Sister Laura's Food, but not for the baby, it was for herself and George to drink. She had bought the food for Joe, but he could not digest it. After trying several alternatives, Nellie had given him Nestlé's milk and was immensely relieved to find that it suited him and he began to thrive.

She was grateful to George's sister, for Martha occasionally sent her cast-off clothes. She would probably have added a few more had she known that Nellie was obliged to wash her vest, knickers and underskirt in the brewhouse and then stand shivering in a blouse and skirt until they dried.

George attempted desperately to find work. With some other men, he set off to cycle to Liverpool. He had just half a crown in his pocket and a few sandwiches, and when they eventually arrived at the docks, they found 2,000 men waiting for 20 jobs. On the return journey, the tyres on the wheels having worn away, the dispirited men had to tie rags around the rims. George also cycled to the Morris Cowley works at Oxford, but it was again a fruitless journey.

When he went to draw his dole money, he learned that a scheme was being offered to the jobless. He put his name down on the waiting list and two months later began to attend the Training Centre at Birmingham to learn bricklaying. He was paid 11s 3d a week and his dinner and fares were provided.

Nellie's wage was £1 0s 9d, out of which she paid Martha 12s 6d for rent and light. After paying Annie 5s for minding Joe, it left them with 14s 6d to live on. A list of prices given here will indicate how difficult Nellie found it to manage on what they had:

| | |
|---|---|
| Margarine | 6d per lb |
| Tea | 4½d per qtr |
| Butter | 1s 3d per lb |
| Potatoes | 6d for 5lb |
| Pork Chops | 10d & 1s 3d per lb |
| Rabbits | 1s 3d each |
| Stewing bits | 6d per lb |
| Onions | 2d per lb |
| Peas in Pod | 3d per lb |
| Lard | 6d per lb |
| Lamb chops | from 9d per lb |
| Cheese | from 1s to 1s 3d per lb |
| Carrots & Parsnips | 3d per lb |
| Neck of Lamb | 8d per lb |
| Breast of Lamb | 2 for 9d |
| Sugar | 4½d for 2lb |
| Pig's Pudding | 6d per lb |
| Faggots | 3d each |
| Danish Bacon | 1s 3d per lb |
| Jam | 6d a jar |
| Streaky Bacon | 9d per lb |
| Fruit Cake | 6d |
| 2lb Loaf | 4½d |
| Custard Pies | 2d |
| Oranges | ½d & 1d |
| Bread Pudding | 1d |
| Eggs | 1s per dozen |
| Fancy Cakes | 2d & 3d |
| Tinned Pineapple | 4½d |
| Oval Blue | 1d |
| Packet of Tea | 2d |
| Fennings Long Healers | 2d |
| Hudson's Soap Powder | 3d |
| Nostralin | 1s 11d |
| Oval Black Lead | 1d |

George's mother gave them nothing, although she must have known how desperate they were. Nellie realised now just how miserable George's life had been before they met. On Joe's first Christmas she had made some decorations and had managed to get a few little

*Joe at Church
Street.*

*Joe with
schoolmates,
front left.*

*George with workmates, far left.*

*George with workmates, far right.*

*George as a foreman with Blackburn & Crosslands. He can be seen on the front row, seventh from the left.*

things for the makeshift tree. Martha had dismissed these preparations as 'a waste of time' and 'all that rubbish'. George told Nellie that never once in his life had his mother decorated a room or bought presents for her children. 'Christmas Day was just the same as any other,' he told her.

When Joe was nearly four years old George found a job at Blackburn & Crosslands at Tettenhall. He began as apprentice bricklayer at 10½d an hour and eventually worked his way up to become General Foreman.

When Joe was five he started to attend St Joseph's School, which adjoined the little shop. Martha had refused to look after the child after school until his mother came home, so Nellie was obliged to give up her job. George was happy about this, saying that she had worked for long enough and anyway they could manage quite well now on his wages.

Nellie preferred to spend much of her time at her mother's rather than stay at home with Martha. She was never idle though, and helped Annie to wash, iron, clean and even wallpaper the house. Nance and George were now married and to Nellie's delight had

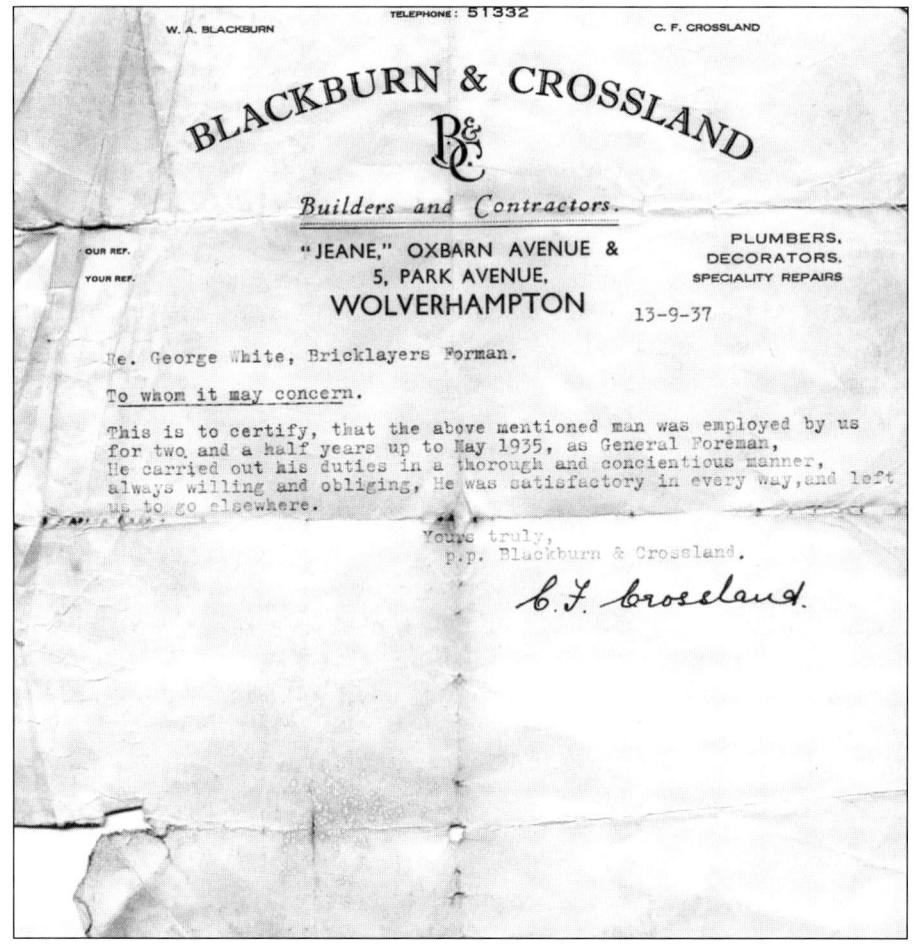

*A letter of reference for George, when he moved on from Blackburn &
Crossland.*

settled just a few doors away next to The George pub. Joe spent a lot
of time with his Aunt Nancy and she made a great fuss of him.

But Nellie was, at times, desperately unhappy. Her mother-in-law
was poisoning her life, constantly trying to cause trouble between
husband and wife. She tried Nellie's patience to the utmost when,
having refused Joe sweets, Martha would take him into the shop and
stuff him with them. It was not easy to obtain council property and
with only one child, Nellie thought how hopeless it was and longed
for a house of her own.

# 23

# A Home of their Own

Joe had just turned six when Nellie was overjoyed to find herself pregnant again. She hoped that this time it would be a girl. 'We'll call her Mary if it is,' she told George happily. Annie reckoned it was about time they had a place of their own too and told Nellie that she would make enquiries and keep her ears open.

But it was Evelyn who brought the news. She was soon to be married and was having a house built in Harrowby Place at Willenhall. She happened to mention to Mrs Rostance, who was having the semi next door, that her sister was hoping for a council house. Mrs Rostance's manner became confidential, 'You tell yer sister as we'll be movin' from Owen Street as soon as this house is ready. We 'aven't told anybody yet as we'm leavin' so your sister can apply straight away.' Evelyn wasted no time in telling Nellie, who discussed it with George and her mother.

Annie offered to go with her to see Councillor Charlie Simmonds. She had once been in service to the family and in fact had been married from his house.

Gripped with excitement, Nellie and her mother went to see him the next day. Charlie obligingly promised to put a word in at Belchers, who collected the council rents. He was able to confirm to a delighted Nellie that it was all arranged and that the council had agreed to offer her the key. Nellie could not believe her luck, at last she would be free to make a proper home for her family.

A few days later, however, Annie was stopped in the street and told that the key to no. 13 Owen Street had been promised to another family, who had offered £20 for it.

Annie was furious. She fetched Nellie and together they sought out Charlie at his coal wharf. He was in his office when they arrived. ''Ello Annie,' he greeted her, 'wot can I do fer you.'

Annie poured out her tale and when she had finished, Charlie was livid. He picked up the phone and rang Belchers. The unfortunate man on the other end must have wondered what had hit him.

*No. 13 Owen Street.*

'Wot about that key you promised Mrs White?' he thundered. Cutting through explanations that the other couple had a prior claim, Charlie informed the man that Mrs White's application had been approved by the council, she would be collecting the key the following Friday, and unless it was handed over, somebody would be 'gooin' ter jail'.

Nellie presented herself at Belchers on the Bull Stake early on Friday morning. When she explained what she had come for, the man skimmed the rent book and the key over the desk at her. The name on the book had been rubbed out and that of George White substituted, but Nellie didn't care about that or about the man's attitude; she had the key and that was all that mattered.

When she told Martha the news, her mother-in-law said sourly, 'My son will never leave me!'

''E can please 'imself,' cried Nellie 'but I'm gooin' if I 'ave ter crawl on me 'ands an' knees to get theer.'

The Rostances were vacating the house the following Saturday at 11 a.m., so George made arrangements to hire Bob Smith's hand cart to move their few bits and pieces.

Heavily pregnant, Nellie could do no heavy lifting, but there were plenty of willing hands.

*George, Joe and Nellie.*

*Annie.*

*George and Joe at Owen Street.*

Her brother, George, Nance, Annie, Evelyn and Marie, all came along to help and by two o'clock that afternoon, the house was ready.

Mrs Rostance had kindly left her net curtains at the front windows and the lino on the stairs. Annie had given them some draw curtains, an armchair, a scrubbed table and a hearth rug.

The two men quickly laid the new lino for the front room, while Marie and Evelyn cleaned the windows.

There was no furniture for the front room, but the smaller kitchen was adequately filled with the white sink underneath the window, a small gas boiler, the table, a black-leaded stove and the small black-leaded fireplace.

There was a bathroom off the kitchen and an outside lavatory and coal place. There were three bedrooms and from the landing window, Nellie could look out onto Bush Park. The view from her bedroom window overlooked the fields adjoining Charles Richards' factory.

When everything had been arranged and the others were departing, George and Nellie waved them off.

Nellie, tired out but entirely contented, smiled at George. 'I think this 'as bin the 'appiest day of me life,' she told him. George put an arm around her shoulders and, with Joe skipping beside them, they walked to the gate. Although the park looked bleak, the trees almost leafless in the late November afternoon, Nellie's thoughts flew to the next summer when, God willing, she, Joe and the new baby would sit there in the warm sunshine.

*Nellie and George in later years.*